GW01339617

NADIA

Marion Connock

of Romania

Duckworth

© 1977 Marion Connock

First published 1977 by
Gerald Duckworth & Co. Ltd.,
The Old Piano Factory,
43 Gloucester Crescent, London NW1

Book design by
Alphabet and Image, Sherborne, Dorset

All rights reserved. No part of this
publication may be reproduced, stored in a
retrieval system, or transmitted, in any
form or by any means, electronic, mechanical,
photocopying, recording or otherwise, without
the prior consent of the publisher.

ISBN: 0 7156 1241 7

Filmset by Keyspools Ltd., Golborne, Lancashire
Printed by Chapel River Press, Andover, Hampshire

CONTENTS

	Acknowledgments	7
	Foreword by Maria Simionescu	9
1	First Glimpse of Nadia	11
2	The Gimnastica at Gheorghiu-Dej	21
3	Towards Competition Standard	29
4	The Challenge of Olga Korbut	41
5	Home Town Triumphant	51
6	European Champion	61
7	The First Ever 'Perfect 10'	73
8	Nadia and Teodora at Home	91
9	Montreal 1976	99
10	Into the Future	121
	Picture Credits	131
	Montreal Olympic Results	132

ACKNOWLEDGMENTS

My sincere thanks are due to the Council of Physical Education and Sports and the Members of the Olympic Committee of the Socialist Republic of Romania for permitting me to be 'la grande exception' among the many people from many countries who wanted to write about Nadia, but had to be refused. It has been a delightful experience and I am very conscious of my good fortune.

It would be difficult to make personal reference to all of those who gave so freely of their time and help, but I must especially thank Ion Paun, Director of the Foreign Relations Department, who arranged for me to go to Gh. Gheorghiu-Dej to meet Nadia in her own environment: Maria Simionescu –Mrs Mili – Vice President of the Technical Committee of the International Gymnastics Federation, whom I fancy did a deal of persuading for me; Gheorghe Poenaru, Director of the Sports Club at Gh. Gheorghiu-Dej who saw to it that I met those who have known Nadia since her early childhood; and Virgil Ludo, sportsman and writer of Brasov, for his charming Romanian hospitality and his encouragement.

I must also thank Barbara Palmer, judge and coach British Amateur Gymnastics Association for her valuable advice. Finally I send my love to Aura Vlad and Cornelia Ionescu of the British Council in Bucharest and my heartfelt thanks for more than I can say.

M.C.

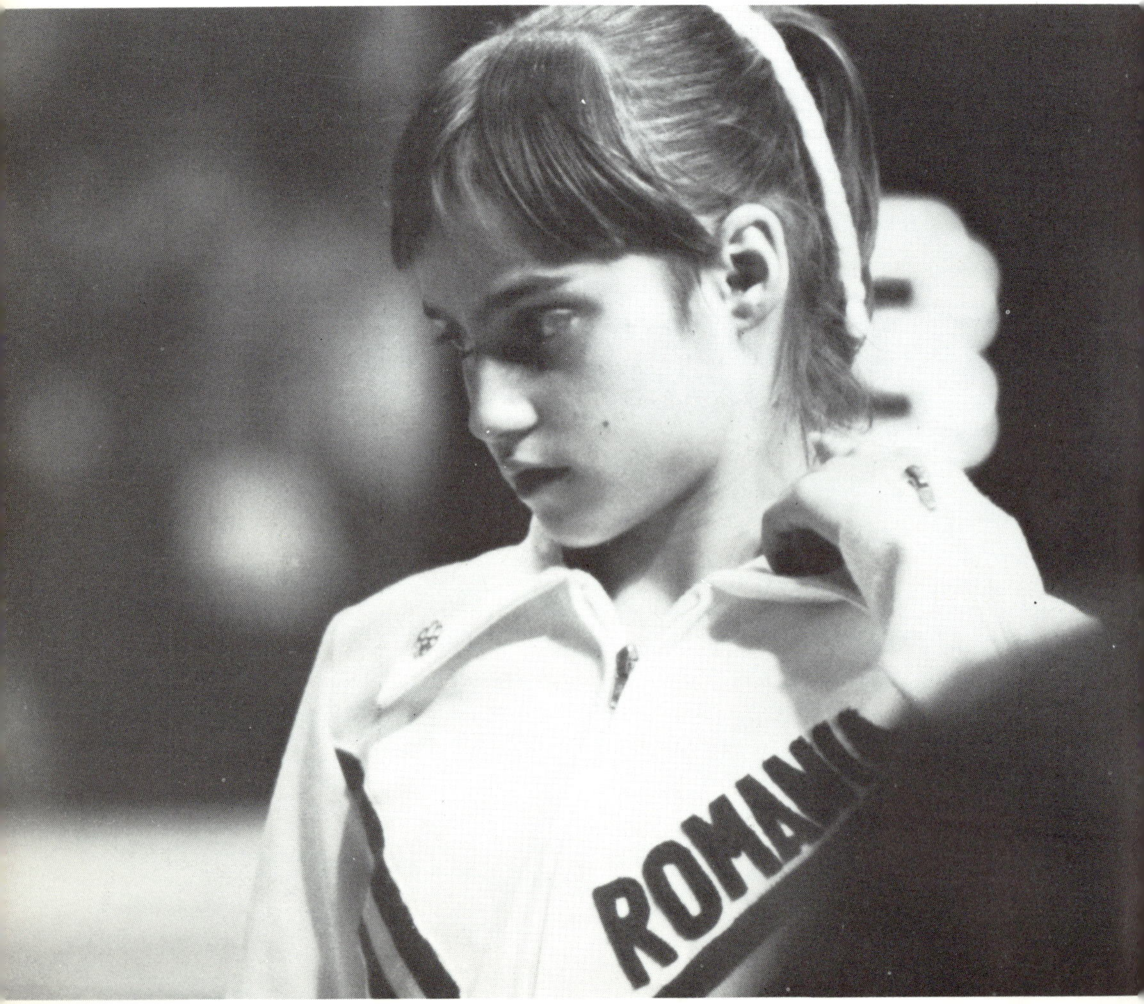
ROMANI

FOREWORD

Nadia Comaneci is the youngest Olympic champion ever. She has a world-class talent. But her achievement is also the fruit of wise selection, the right conditions and systematic early training. From the circle of her team mates, her coaches and the school in which she studies, Nadia has risen to become what she is today: a girl who revolutionized the sport to which she has dedicated herself completely.

Marion Connock's book is a human document. It shows Nadia as she is – a girl like any other, with her own personality, her own hopes and wishes, her own little upsets, who feels most at home among her own family. To the world she is a prodigy, but for me she is also the fulfilment of a concept which governed our whole activity.

Gymnastics is a beautiful sport that requires many years of practice. It will take time for it to establish its own traditions, but perhaps one day its popularity will challenge that of football, boxing and other sports that already command a huge following. Nadia has made an amazing contribution to the spread of gymnastics among children and young people throughout the world, showing that even a young person may reach the highest place in the Olympic pantheon.

To the industrious and warm-hearted people of Romania, Nadia is a new star in her country's golden crown.

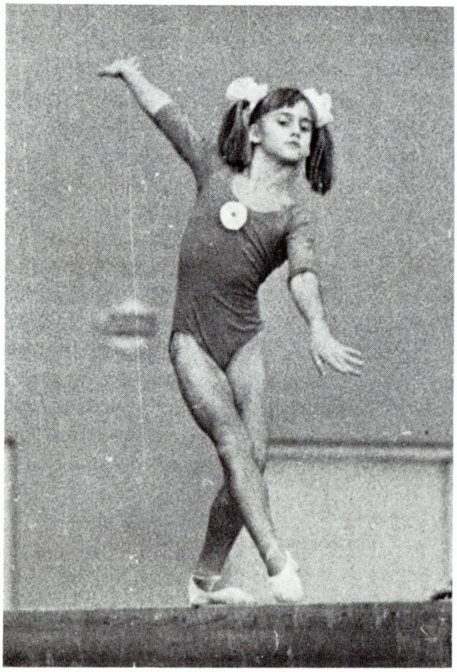

1 FIRST GLIMPSE OF NADIA

Nadia Comaneci was only three years old when, in 1965, the Romanian Peoples' Republic sought to honour the memory of their first President by giving his name to the town in which she was born.

Planned to provide homes for the workers of the giant petrochemical complex eight kilometres away, it had been built on the site of the birthplace of Stephen the Great, Voivode of Moldavia in the fifteenth century. Thus it was that – with history seeming to link two esteemed leaders, the one of the past and the other of the new regime – the ancient town of Onesti became the municipality of Gheorghe Gheorghiu-Dej.

But, amid the crowd of eager spectators who filled the sports stadium for the dedication ceremony, the small girl, with white ribbon bows perched like butterflies on either side of her solemn face, would no doubt have attracted little more than a passing glance as she endeavoured to free herself from her father's restraining arms. For nobody was to know that, at the tender age of fourteen, she was to bring so much renown to her country that, at a splendid reception in the Palace of Sports and Culture in Bucharest, Nicolae Ceauşescu, the President of Romania, would invest her with one of the highest orders of the land, the Gold Medal of a Hero of Socialist Labour.

* * * * * *

It was happy news for the newly married Gheorghe and Stefania Comaneci when, in the early spring of 1961, Stefania knew that they were to have their first child. Going to see a Russian film by way of celebration, Stefania was entranced with its lovely heroine and decided that if the baby was a girl, it was to be called Nadia after her. Gheorghe was not so sure; he wanted a boy, who was to be called Adrian . . .

First glimpse of Nadia

It was a girl.

But if Gheorghe was disappointed he certainly did not show it when, on 12 November, he tiptoed in to see the little daughter whose arrival had coincided with the first of the winter snows – Nadia Elena Comaneci. With her deep-blue eyes and tiny waving fists he thought her the most beautiful baby in the world. He was not to know that eyes of that depth can change and that Nadia's were to become even more attractive as they turned to a brown which would better be described as bronze, and which, in the years ahead, were to add to the contemplative look of a naturally serious girl.

It was not long, however, before the new addition to the family began to be a problem to her mother. The most restless and energetic child imaginable, she was only a few months old when she kicked the covers off her pram or pulled herself up to bounce, so that she had it rocking dangerously. She walked early, and with a frown of determination that was absurd on her baby face she would climb upon anything to reach what attracted her. Stefania was afraid to leave her for a moment, but Gheorghe found it amusing. Thrilled with her daring, he would only laugh as he caught and tossed her in his arms.

Nadia was barely three when Stefania began to worry that there seemed to be nothing of the femininity she had looked for in the daughter she had wanted so much. Nadia was very independent and, except for the rare occasions when she would fling herself at her mother and cling closely for a bit of loving, she wanted only to be out on the patch of grass that was the children's playground, to do handstands or kick a ball around with the boys. Sometimes they found her a nuisance, but at others it was fun to teach the tiny mite the acrobatics they were learning at school. Left to herself, Nadia would practise them with a tenacity that seemed to have her more often upside down than on her feet.

Hoping that school would use up much of her excess energy, her parents could scarcely wait for her third birthday when she would be starting at the kindergarten which, in Romania, is considered to be a vital period in a child's education. As in nursery schools everywhere, lessons are little more than play, but at this early age they are introduced to their national fairy tales and folklore, and their pride in their country is awakened.

Since many children do not have a grandmother to care for them during their mother's working hours – for all women work in Romania – they are used to being left during the day at a creche. Going to a kindergarten at three years old is therefore something they

First glimpse of Nadia

accept as naturally as going to an exciting second home. By the time they are old enough to go on to junior schools, their upbringing has developed in them a sense of independence that has them living in two worlds – the world of home, where the child's love for his parents is in no way diminished; and the world of school, where he is responsible to himself and to his country for his progress.

Nadia revelled in the kindergarten, especially the games and the fairy stories. Still a serious child, though never an unhappy one, she mixed freely enough with the other children, even if she made no special friends. Once back at home, however, there was no holding her, for as soon as Stefania's back was turned she would be off in a

Gymnasts in the making

flash. Luckily, with few people owning cars and no taxis in Gheorghiu-Dej, there was little traffic, even on the main Boulevards, while in the grass-bordered avenues in which the blocks of flats are situated, there was hardly any at all. Nadia would be looking for the boys, for there never was a time in the daylight hours, except at school, when there was not sport of some kind or another going on. If it was not the gymnastics which she adored, there would surely be a game of football. Romania had become one of the most sports-conscious countries in Europe, and in the interests of the health of the nation every school included physical training in its curriculum. Even the smallest of the little fellows with whom Nadia played saw himself as a future super-athlete. They could hardly wait to be big enough to go to

First glimpse of Nadia

First glimpse of Nadia

the Sports Club to train, even though every school was provided with its necessary equipment.

Romania certainly takes her sports seriously, and there are comprehensive sports clubs and fine stadiums in every major city up and down the country. It is not surprising that in the comparatively short time in which they have been serious contenders in the International arena, the Romanians came fifth on the medal list at the Montreal Olympics, with only the USSR, the USA and East and West Germany ahead of them, out of the forty-eight countries which competed.

But that was way ahead and Nadia was still at the kindergarten when, in 1965, a team of fifty gymnasts was formed at the Sports Club with the hope that some of its brighter stars would add to the national titles it was hoped to win for the honour of Gheorghiu-Dej. Called 'The Flame', the team was divided into two groups, in the second of which the youngest and one of the most promising members was a little girl of 8, Anca Grigoras.

But Anca was by no means the youngest of the children who spent her free time in a 'gimnastica'. Away in a mining village in the Carpathian Mountains, there were six- and seven-year-olds who would one day be able to boast that they had been the first pupils of the famous Bela and Marta Karoly.

A blonde, blue-eyed young giant of Hungarian descent but, like his parents before him, born in Romania, Bela Karoly had been in his early twenties when he married his pretty, dark-haired Marta. Bela was an all-round sportsman and Marta a dedicated gymnast with the concentration on technical detail that makes for perfection. Marta was excited with the new approach to women's gymnastics, which gave it something of the appeal of ballet, with added grace and a greater opportunity for imaginative interpretation. And, with the memory of the bronze medal that the Romanian team had won at the Rome Olympics to inspire her, she had original ideas for the finding and training of future champions.

Agreeing with Professor Gheorghe Chisoiu – considered to be a leading authority on gymnastics in Romania – that girls should begin their training at between $5\frac{1}{2}$ and 7, she planned to teach them the first elements of posture, balance and muscular control when they had a puppy's loose-limbed agility and little or no sense of fear; and before they were old enough to tighten up and develop faults which would be difficult to cure.

Bela had a loving faith in Marta and readily agreed that they

A secondary school in Bucharest shows gymnastics akin to ballet

15

First glimpse of Nadia

One of the selecti takes her first steps on the beam

should search among the kindergartens for the children who could prove her right. It was the beginning of a partnership that, because of the differing qualities and expertise that each could bring to it, has been a splendid success.

The little girls they found learned from Marta how to stand with a poised dignity at the end of the beam, before their small feet, placed heel in front of toe, felt their way across it: and how to put just sufficient impetus into the spring so that they could stand straight and taut on their hands, with their legs beautifully together before parting into the ever-widening 'V' that would have them horizontal. Meanwhile Bela, the gentle disciplinarian, instilled in them the confidence to be just a little more venturesome, secure in the knowledge that his strong arms were there to catch them.

Starting in a special school at Vulcan, near Brasov, the Karolys went on to a sports school at Petrosani before coming to Gheorghiu-Dej in 1967, at the behest of Mrs Maria Simionescu, to undertake the training of the keen members of 'The Flame' at the 'Onesti' Sports Club. But it was not until February 1968 that Bela and Marta set out to add to the group with forty children of their own choosing from the kindergartens, among whom were Mariana Cojanu, Georgeta Gabor, Gabriela Sabadiş, Viorica Dumitriu, Ionela Burlacu and Nadia Comaneci – who was at this time just six years old.

First glimpse of Nadia

It was wonderfully exciting for Nadia to know that she was to learn how to become a real gymnast like Anca Grigoras, and she rushed home to tell her mother and the new baby. . . .

This time it had been the son for whom her father had hoped, even though she had heard her mother tell him, ruefully, that he already had one in his tomboy daughter. For the kindergarten had done little to change Nadia, who still liked nothing better than to play with the boys in the street. She had no close friends but would laugh and joke with children as she never would with her teachers or with those whom she regarded as 'grown-ups'. With them she was unfailingly polite, but she would seem to retire into herself, answering questions with monosyllables and a searching look that was disconcerting in those strange, unfathomable eyes. She could, perhaps, have been likened to Peter Pan – a fey little creature with a life apart.

She was just seven and a half and had left the kindergarten for her 'general' school, when Gheorghe and Stefania heard that her training with the Karolys had brought her to a standard which warranted her transfer to the second class of the splendid new Gimnastica High School of which everyone was talking.

Secrets shared by future stars. Nadia Comaneci talks to Georgeta Gabor.

First glimpse of Nadia

The ultra-modern Gimnastica was started in 1968. It is now identified with the world's most famous gymnastic team.

The new Gimnastica, with its school and boarding hostel, was the dream-come-true of Maria Emilia Simionescu, the administrative head of women's technical gymnastics in Romania. Known and loved by gymnasts throughout the country as 'Mrs Mili', she had been the Romanian Coach at the Melbourne, Rome and Tokyo Olympics and was to be an International judge at Munich in 1972 and Montreal in 1976. Convinced that the right training conditions could produce Romanian gymnasts as good as, or better than, any to be found in Europe, Mili was determined to prove it. She had sought to do so by establishing a central gimnastica at Gheorghiu-Dej which could take promising children of 6 or 7 and other established gymnasts from all over the country who needed a more specialized training, and combine training with a first-class education. The lucky 'tinies' would be selected annually by a competitive examination in September, at the beginning of the school year.

This was a new idea for gymnastics. There were already similar schools for children who showed promise in the arts – the potential musicians, artists, and so on – and this had no doubt helped to persuade the National Council for Physical Education and Sport that they were lagging behind. But those who know Mili Simionescu

First glimpse of Nadia

will say that it was the sincerity of her faith in what she believed could give something of value to the country that won the day for her.

It was on one of her periodic visits to inspect the progress of The Flame, when the construction of the new gymnasium was already well-advanced, that Mrs Mili had her first glimpse of Nadia among the Karolys' forty young newcomers. And today, looking back, she likes to remember that she was one of the few who had sensed 'something different' in the little girl which, added to her remarkable tenacity, could take her to the very top.

Making an impression on her instructors – the image of Nadia at 8 years old.

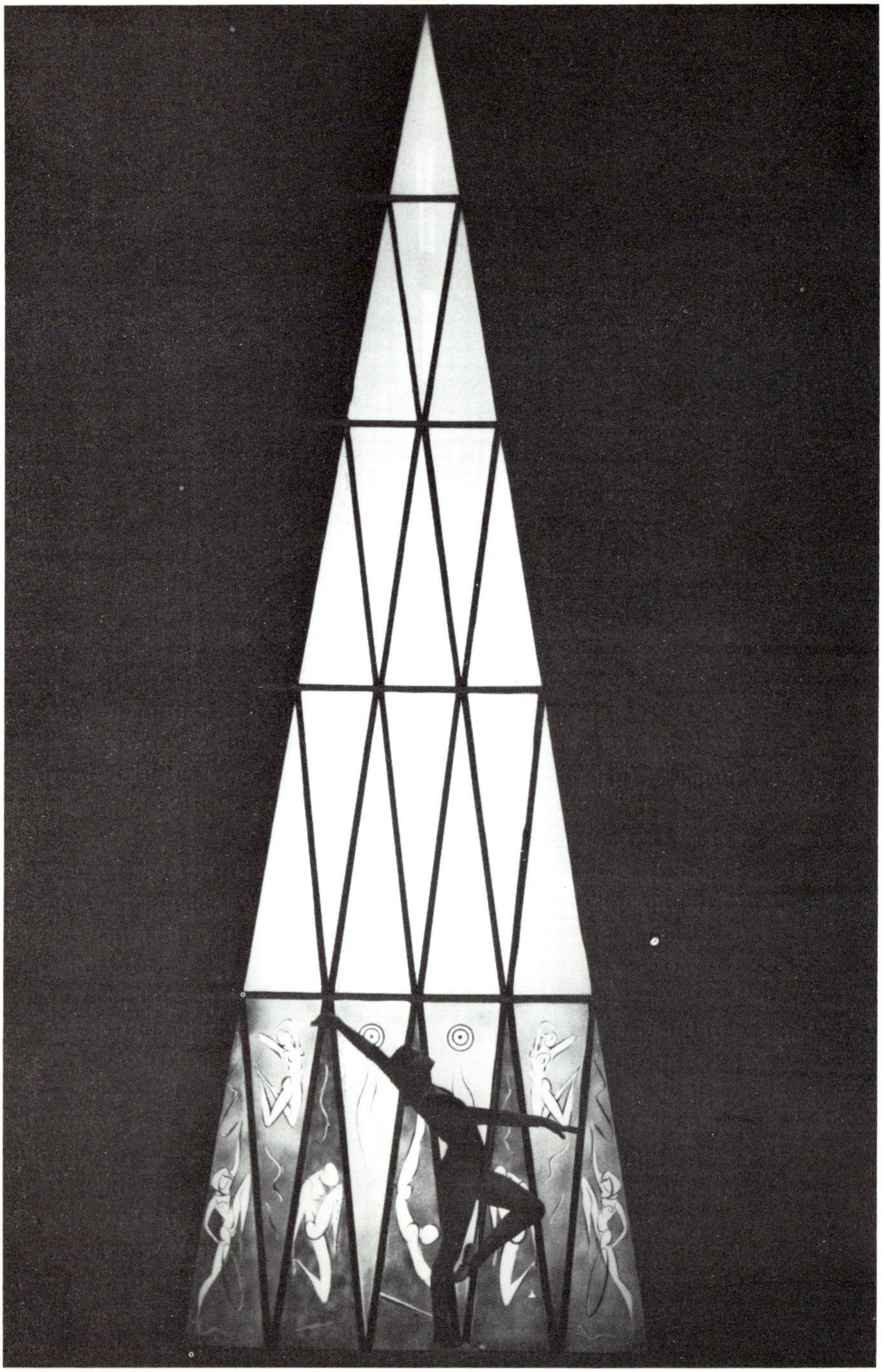

2 THE GIMNASTICA AT GHEORGHIU-DEJ

The Gimnastica was opened at Gheorghiu-Dej in 1969. It had all the facilities for the specialized training of gymnasts to a standard that would not only present a challenge to young enthusiasts all over the country, but blaze a trail for Romania throughout the world.

The ultra-modern gymnasium had sixteen highly trained professors,* and its own doctors, choreographer and pianists. It had been designed to have a considerable amount of apparatus and floor-training in progress at the same time. At one end was a velvet-soft twelve-metre square, a flowing expanse of pale green in front of the bar and wall mirrors. At the other were rows of four-inch beams beside the asymmetrical bars. A corridor in front of the strange, triangular-shaped windows provided the run that was needed for vaulting the horse.

Within easy walking distance was the boarding hostel and the Gimnastica High School. The school, with its own complement of professors of various subjects working under a headmaster and his assistant, the headmistress, was ready to receive up to 380 pupils.

With a number of the well-established older members of the disbanded Flame qualifying for admission, it was planned to hold the first 'Selecte' in September for the six- and seven-year-olds, who were to be strictly limited to 85 a year.

Mrs Mili was there among the judges, and she was not in the least surprised that there should be hundreds of young aspirants waiting hopefully to show what they could do. As they arrived in small groups from the changing rooms, they looked enchanting in their red or blue leotards, their well-brushed hair tied with the traditional

A futuristic window in the Gimnastica

* In Romania a university or teaching degree automatically confers the title of 'Professor'.

The excitement of selection for young hopefuls

white ribbons – for, white being a sign of purity, no little girl in Romania is ever to be seen with a coloured ribbon.

Mrs Mili found it sad that so many would have to be turned away.

But judges, steeling their hearts, have to guard against being influenced by an appealing little face or an attractive personality; there has to be so much more. Not only must the essential physical attributes be there of a strong and resilient body, but there must be a keen intelligence and evidence of a mental stability sufficient to withstand the monotony of years of concentrated and arduous training. Also, the child must satisfy those whose decision will determine her future, that she has the dedication and courage needed to master the seemingly impossible.

Among the successful ones this time was young Dana Craciun, who is being coached by Florin and Florica Dobre, two of the top trainers at Gheorghiu-Dej. Much is expected of her in the future. She was proud indeed to be given her new identity card which, with a small photograph in the top left-hand corner and the usual details of date and place of birth, was the proof that she had been officially accepted as a trainee of the new Gheorghiu-Dej Gimnastica. She was proud too of the little book she was given, which would record every detail of her training and her successes or failures, endorsed with the official stamp.

A junior line-up

The beginning of that winter term of 1969 – little more than a month before her eighth birthday – was the start of a routine for Nadia. Her hours would now be carefully programmed between lessons at the new school and training periods at the gym. For the newest, very young children, training was limited to two hours a day, but for Nadia and the others, who were already experienced and likely to be chosen for the junior team, it was three, and sometimes three-and-a-half hours, with most of the extra time spent with Bela on the apparatus. Not a moment was wasted and, with Bela insisting on absolute punctuality, one had to be on time for everything, including compulsory rest-periods or meals.

Dinner was usually eaten with the boarders at the hostels to maintain the diet that had been carefully worked out by nutritionists to keep the young gymnasts fit and strong without giving them excess weight. They could eat as much as they liked of protein foods, which were there for them in abundance – meat (excluding pork), fish, poultry, cheese and eggs – and they were encouraged to eat lots of green vegetables, salads and fresh fruit, and to drink as much milk as they could take. Only starch was frowned upon – bread, potatoes, biscuits, cakes, chocolates, sweets and too much ice-cream. Stefania says it was strange the children never seemed to miss them. But none of their friends ate them, so, scarcely ever seeing them, they never

The beginning of a special relationship. Bela Karoly watches an important pupil with a keen eye. Nadia looks to him for guidance, and listens.

thought of them. Maybe it helped that, while boxes of chocolates can be bought in the cake shops in Gheorghiu-Dej, there are no sweet shops such as abound in the West. The nearest thing that could be said to present a temptation was the cream cakes in the patisseries.

It was a life of strict discipline, to which Nadia was quick to adapt herself – almost as if, young as she was, she saw it as the means of fulfilling the urge she had had since babyhood to master what appeared beyond her reach. There was a difference, too, in her attitude to her training, for while she had always been obedient during the odd hours she spent there, often there was something oddly elusive about her, when, with a moment free, she would be concentrating, with an even greater effort, on a movement or feat of her own invention. She was essentially an individualist. But now with her eyes fixed upon Bela or Marta, she listened intently to their every word, as though she could never hear enough. She loved every moment, including the daily routine training, which might have become irksome. First there would be the warming up with the 'follow my leader' running and skipping and springing into the air in a circle on the large green square. It was an honour to be chosen by Marta as the leader, since it meant that you were one of the best. The pianist would be playing a gay tune. Arms would be flung upwards or sideways as you went, with fingers outstretched in just the right position – the first, third and fourth stretched straight, with the second pointing down and the thumb lying smoothly along the palm. Then would come the one, two, three skips and, with the balance evenly divided between the legs, a sweeping down to touch the floor – or,

The Gimnastica at Gheorghiu-Dej

with another change, a run of one, two, three and a leap into the air with arms stretching up and legs parting widely into a horizontal split. Nadia loved this one, it was exhilarating! Then more skips, the knees taking it in turn to bend up and up towards the chin – this one to train the knees to tuck themselves up as high as possible in a somersault.

There were many routines, all carefully designed to be of use in specialized feats. And once one was really loosened up, there would be the exercises at the bar in front of the mirror – the leg-swinging, the *grand battement*, the *battement tendu* and the arabesques, with arm movements similar to those of a ballerina.

Then it would be back to the square for exercising every muscle in turn: first the fingers; then the hands, arms, shoulders, neck and head; then body-bending and leg-stretching. Next there would be flips and somersaults diagonally across the velvety softness of the floor: and then special combinations of floor exercises under the direction of Geza Poszar, the tall, dark, clever choreographer, to music that was exactly right from Stabişevschi who, a fine swimming professor, is an even better pianist.

Finally would come the sessions with Marta on the four-inch beam, and with Bela on the asymmetrical bars and the horse. These were the most wonderful of all for Nadia, whose fierce determination never to be beaten by anything that the others could do – especially Mariana Cojanu, for whom it was known that Bela had great hopes – both delighted and amused her trainers. There was nothing the child would not try. She was confident that with Bela, a great disciplinarian, she need never be afraid. His was the eagle eye that watched for the slightest error of judgment; his the unfailing strength, not only to catch her, but to hold her to correct a position at any point of the exercise.

That first busy year at her new school and at the Gimnastica passed quickly. It was a happy girl who, proud of the progress report in her official book, set off for a summer holiday at the seaside with her father and mother and three-year-old brother Adrian.

It was a long journey to the Black Sea, and Adrian, who spent the first hours with his rosy little face pressed to the window as the long train went speeding southwards, had to be wakened for the final change that would take them to Mamaia. Just four miles away from the port of Constanta, with its new harbour, busy with trade, is Mamaia – perhaps the most popular of all the many seaside resorts along the beautiful coast.

There were special delights for all the family. For Gheorghe, an engineer mechanic in a large and noisy garage, it was enough just to lie on the beach during the long hours of sunshine and to watch, through half-closed eyes, his son building endless sand castles; and he would voice sleepy protests to his young daughter when she ran dripping from the sea to urge him to come and play football. For Stefania it was a joy to stroll through the flowers that grew in profusion in the parks and around the nearby fresh-water lagoon, making a splash of colour along the promenade.

But all too soon it was over. Back to Gheorghiu-Dej. Nadia was once again playing with the boys in the streets and longing for the new term to begin. The next year promised to start her on the first steps of a career which, young as she was, she had determined to follow – that of a top gymnast.

Gheorghe Comaneci, Nadia's father

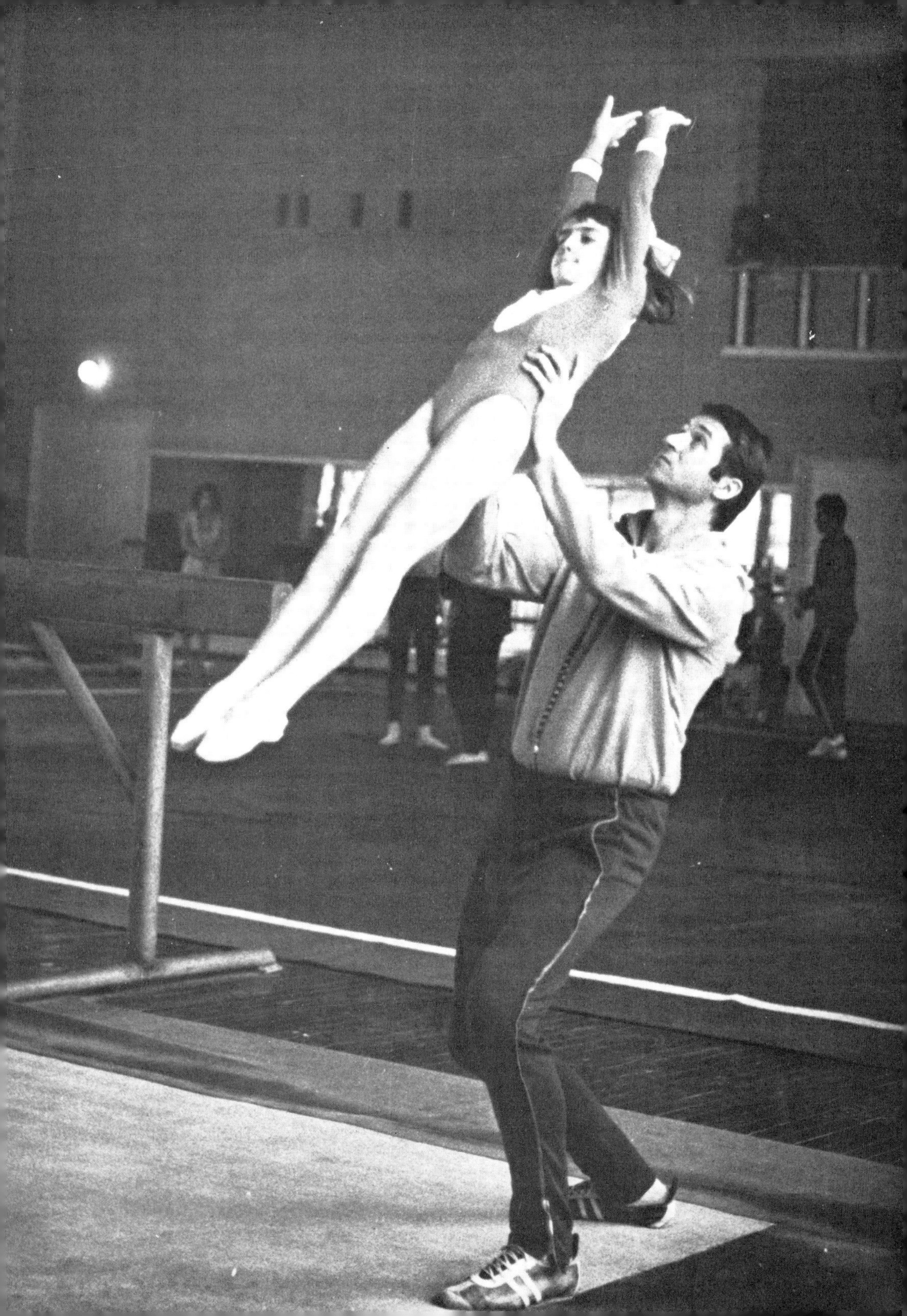

The Gimnastica at Gheorghiu-Dej

Bela would be selecting the team for the fourth-category contest at Sibiu – another of the important gymnastic centres of the country. She had to show him that, in keeping up her exercises during the long holiday, she had lost nothing of her suppleness or skill. Brooding over it in secret – rather than talk it over even with her mother – she imagined her only serious rival in Bela's estimation to be Mariana Cojanu. The others – Viorica Dumitriu and Constanta Dilimot – were good, but she could be better.

But she had reckoned without Teodora Ungureanu.

A year – but for a day – older than Nadia, Teodora had been training with Andrei Kerenkes in Reşiţa – an old metalworking town in the west of Romania near the Yugoslav frontier. Having already proved her worth in a third-category contest, Teodora had been a likely choice for more concentrated training, and Bela Karoly was happy to have her.

Arriving with the rest of the September intake, Teodora was to board at the hostel until such time as her widowed mother, Emilia, could obtain the transfer from her work that would permit her to make a new home for them both in Gheorghiu-Dej.

A pretty girl, Teodora has a certain physical resemblance to Nadia which might make one think them sisters, but here the likeness ceases; for, with one a gay, laughter-loving extrovert and the other serious and reserved, the only thing that was obvious in them both was a dedication to their careers as gymnasts, and a courage and determination to win which had them fighting for supremacy from the very start.

With nothing to suggest that they could be anything other than rivals, it came as a surprise to everyone that, while each of them seemed to give to the other what she most needed, the two little girls immediately became the greatest friends.

Teodora – a new face at the Gimnastica

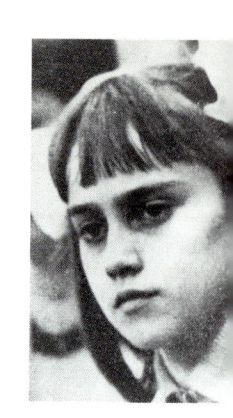

3 TOWARDS COMPETITION STANDARD

Towering over his junior team of five small girls, Bela Karoly was delighted with their first victory at the important gymnastic centre of Sibiu. Though it was a fourth-category* contest, in which they had met with stiff opposition, the children had won easily. Teodora had achieved the highest total, with Mariana a close second, Nadia third and Viorica and Constanta fourth and fifth. Promising them a picnic by way of celebration, Bela and Marta were happy with their excited chatter as they shepherded them back to Gheorghiu-Dej, and full of pride as the girls alighted from the train clutching the bags that contained their leotards and gym shoes.

But hardly had they rushed off to spread the good news than Bela was turning to Marta to discuss the all-important details of their next campaign. Bela was naturally ambitious and very conscious of his responsibility as top trainer. He was as anxious as Mili Simionescu herself that the Gimnastica should justify all that had gone into its founding, and he was already planning to put Gheorghiu-Dej in the forefront of the many gymnastic centres in the country as soon as possible. It would be hard going, and the girls must be kept fit and happy to accomplish it, but with careful selection and training of the talent that was now a continuous flow, together with the talent that was already there to cover the four categories, he considered that in four or five years they could compete with even the more experienced clubs, such as Dinamo, Ploesti and Tineretuliu. Apart from the team successes, he sought to achieve individual national championships and – one day maybe – even international ones.

* Category 1 – under 16. Category 2 – under 14. Category 3 – under 12. Category 4 – under 10.

Towards competition standard

Walking home with Marta, he recalled the moment in the train when he had suddenly become aware of the intensity of Nadia's sombre brown eyes as they were fixed upon him.

'You did well, Nadia,' he had told her. 'Keep it up and you'll do even better.'

Nadia had made no comment, and in her usual way of never letting her face reveal her feelings – remarkable in one so young – had turned away with a brief nod to acknowledge his encouragement. Only she knew that she was by no means satisfied with the performance that had seen her beaten by both Teodora and Mariana. It was not that she grudged her companions their success; on the contrary she was glad for them. Jealousy, as such, had no place in her make-up. Rather it was an impatience with her own inadequacy and the need to prove to herself – more even than to Bela and Marta – that nothing others could achieve was beyond her. As she gazed at Bela, she had been speculating about where she had gone wrong and looking forward to the time when he would be able to tell her and put it right.

But even greater than her preoccupation with the challenge of Teodora and Mariana, was the fascination that her first official contest had had for her, when she was not yet nine years old. Until today competition had been limited to gymnastics at Gheorghiu-Dej. She was only vaguely aware of all that lay beyond in the centres that Anca Grigoras and others of the seniors had visited for contests. It had taken their own contest at Sibiu to bring it home to her that there were other girls in the country, besides those around her, who, like herself, were aiming to become top gymnasts – and maybe not only in Romania, but all over the world. That was what Bela and Marta meant when they talked of international competitions.

Gheorghiu-Dej was not a very big town – not like Moscow or London or Paris or any of the other capital cities they learned about at school. It was not nearly as big as their own Bucharest. How good *were* they, all those girls out there? Were they already doing harder things than she was? She had to find out. . . .

It was a serious question, and she discussed it with Teodora, from whom she was now practically inseparable. From then on, Stefania says, the two small girls seemed to live only for the time they spent in the gym. As they sat on Nadia's bed, nursing the dolls for whom Nadia had hitherto had little use, their talk would be only of the day's mistakes or achievements. Without even being aware of it, Nadia had

Bela and Nadia take the well-worn path from the hostel to the Gimnastica

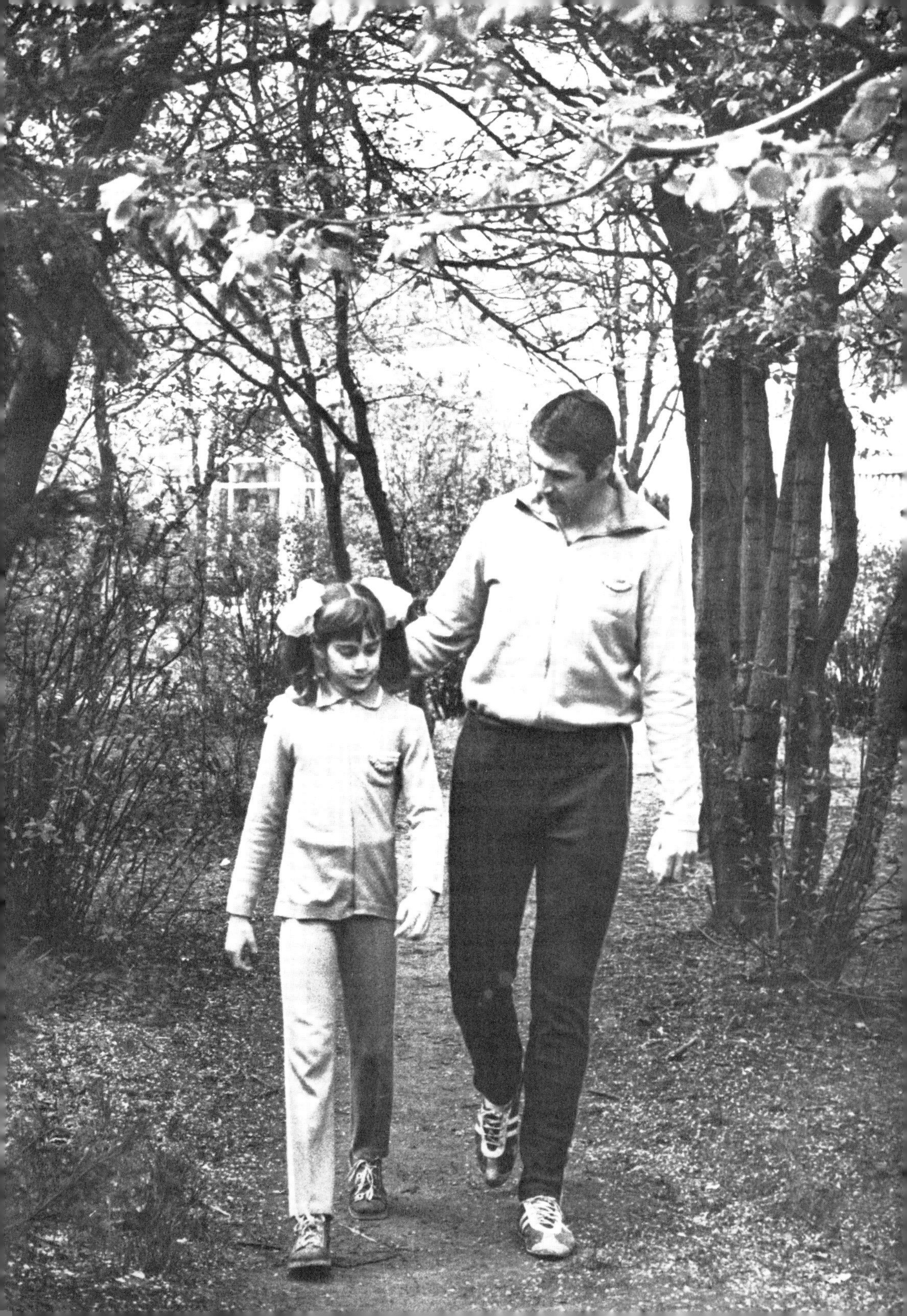

Gheorghiu-Dej

A track-suited Nadia outside her school

Towards competition standard

not only rededicated herself to her training, but increased the friendly rivalry between herself and Teodora. This speeded their progress at a rate that made everyone astonished and delighted.

But though it was not a big town as towns go, Gheorghiu-Dej had grown considerably since its conception in 1953. Set in a valley amid undulating hills and overlooking the meeting of the rivers Oituz and Trotus it was a beautiful town. With the ultra-modernity of the municipal buildings and the blocks of flats designed to give an equal standard of housing to everybody, it could so easily have been stark in its newness and concrete uniformity. But it wasn't. The Romanians are one of the most flower-loving nations in the world, and the place is a mass of colour, resembling nothing so much as a garden city. Flowers and young trees, growing with the town, border the streets and make a central line down each of the two main thoroughfares, the Boulevards Republicii and the Oituz. And, as if that were not enough, flowers encircle the blocks of flats and bloom in window boxes everywhere.

Teodora loved it and could scarcely wait for her mother to come to make a home of their own – though she loyally insisted to Nadia that Reşiţa, also, had many new and impressive buildings.

It was 1971. The spring term had started, after the Christmas holidays, and Nadia was now nine years old. She was in the fourth class at school and was learning both French and English. She wasn't as good at them as Georgeta Gabor, who loved languages – but Georgeta, after all, was cleverer than any of them and always had the best marks. Gheorghe thought Nadia should be concentrating more on her lessons and less on her gym. But her report had been good, and Mrs Pop, the headmistress, had been pleased with her.

It was strange that, with the New Year, there seemed at the same time to be a new air of urgency and excitement in the Gimnastica. It was not that Bela was any different. He had always been a strict disciplinarian and an exacting taskmaster, and he was there waiting for them on that first day, seeming to dare them to be unpunctual. All the girls who had started their gymnastics with Nadia had now arrived at competition standard, and everyone knew that Bela would have been busy planning during the holiday just what contests they would be entering. He would be choosing his teams accordingly. They just had to wait for him to tell them what he had decided.

To her great delight Nadia was to go to Ljubljana in July for her first international. She was to be in a team of seven with Mariana, Viorica, Constanta – who had been with her at Sibiu – Georgeta

Towards competition standard

Gabor, Ana Barcan and Gabriela Sabadiş. July seemed a long way off, but there was a great deal to do. Most of the rehearsing for the compulsory disciplines* would be done as a team, but for each of the girls there had to be a special plotting of her voluntary disciplines – especially those for the floor, when Marta would need to confer with Geza Poszar as to the seven 'difficulties' (with three of them agility sequences).† These had to be incorporated into Poszar's choreography and selected by Marta as those most suited to the girl's capabilities. With these agreed, Poszar would go to Carol Stabişevschi for the two of them to evolve a combination of music and movement expressive of each girl's personality, so as to lend a natural spontaneity and charm to her performance.

Thinking ahead to the many important contests for which he intended to enter the girls, Bela thought the time had come when he must prepare them for the vastly different atmosphere of a large and crowded competitive arena. They had been taught from their earliest days to walk with poise and dignity, both towards and away from the positioning place of a discipline, and Bela need never fear that a lack of grace from any one of them would alienate the five judges. Rather he hoped to instil in them, while they were still very young, a confidence that would allow them to disregard an audience and concentrate solely on what they set out to do. First, to stand immobile until the judges showed they were ready, as the red light changed to green; secondly, to present themselves to the Master Judge, who would be sitting in the centre; finally, to forget everything except that Marta was there watching and that it was as easy to perform there as in the Gimnastica.

If he felt that one of his teams needed isolated coaching, Bela would sometimes take them as a small treat to a gym in Brasov. At this time of year the Carpathians were still covered with snow, and winter sports would be included in the girls' curriculum. They loved it all, especially the ski-ing, and soon became quite skilled. At such times Bela was a lot of fun – just as he was at the picnics that he and Marta organized, and when they played football. Marta's team invariably won, since they would have Teodora as a forward. With her speed and fine footwork she was practically unbeatable.

With the contest at Partizan Ljubljana at the beginning of the summer holidays, school had already finished, so they were able to

---

* The gymnastic term for exercises.
† A typical agility sequence could be: Round off, flick-flac, stretched jump with 180° turn into somersault forward (arabian forward) round off, stretched somersault backwards.

Nadia in action on the asymmetrical bars

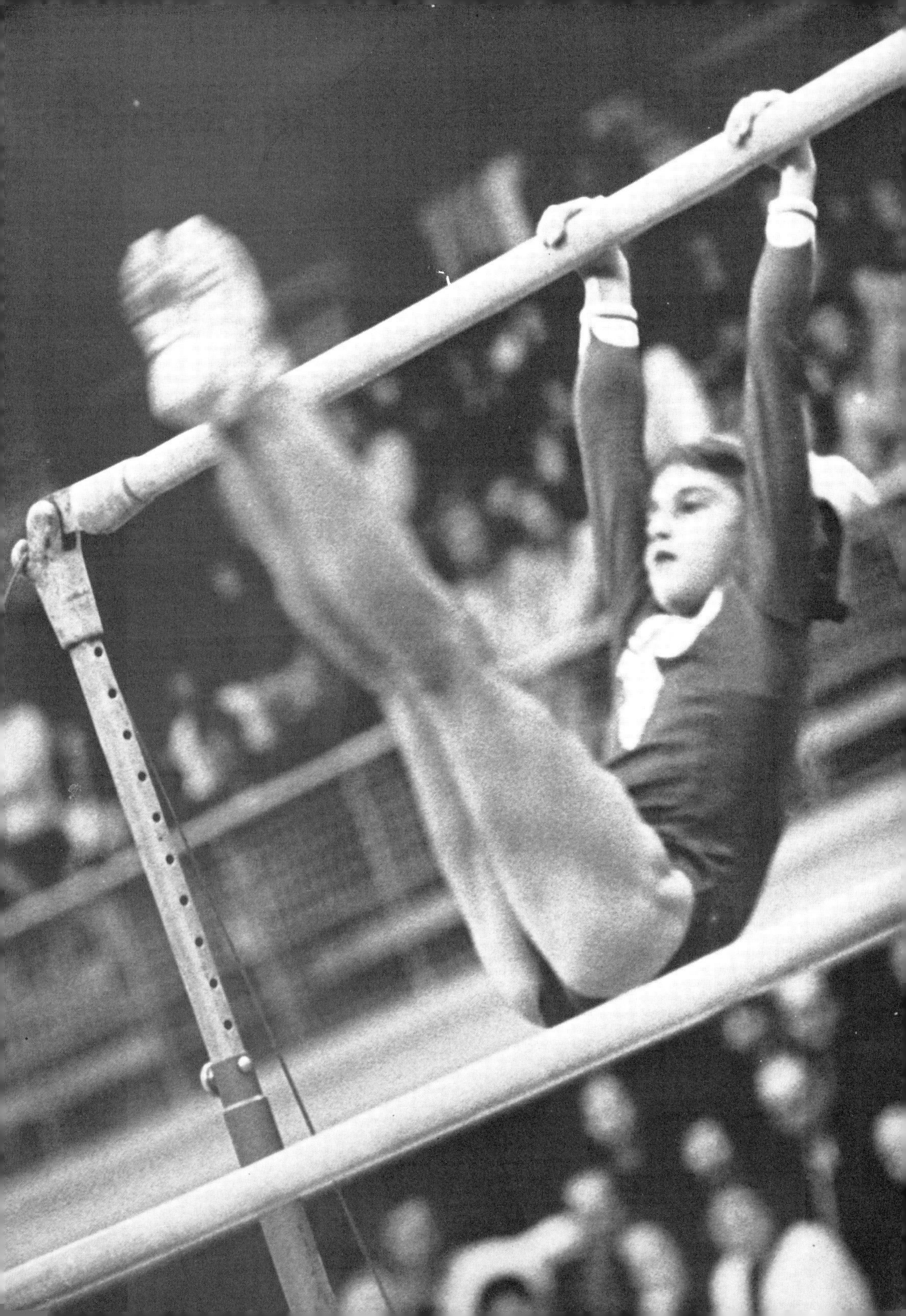

Towards competition standard

linger at the Sports Club after final rehearsals at the gym, to watch the tennis or handball, or even the young canoeists training on the river. Nadia could never have enough of any sport.

The all-important adventure, however, promised to be not only the contest for which they had been working hard, but the journey across Yugoslavia – almost as far as the borders of Italy and Austria. The girls against whom they would be competing would speak another language.

With their things already packed, they each had pocket money donated by parents, grandparents and friends and were the envy of all their friends. Nadia had been a little sad that Teodora was not to be with them. But, as she was a year older, Bela had other ideas for her in the second and third categories. There was also the fact that, while she was undoubtedly one of the most promising of all the many outstanding young gymnasts, and certainly one of the most courageous, Teodora had not yet found the strength of will that enabled Nadia to become oblivious of an audience. A sudden attack of nerves could mar Teodora's performance. Bela and Marta were just hoping that she would become more confident. But it was Mrs Mili who tackled her on the subject.

'What do you think of competing in international competitions, Teodora?' she asked. 'Do you think you could be brave enough?'

'Only with Nadia,' came the reply.

The trip was a splendid success. The initial shyness in the changing rooms quickly changed to peals of friendly laughter as the girls of the two adjoining countries tried to make themselves understood.

The result was a win for the team from Gheorghiu-Dej. Nadia came first this time, with a total of 38.50 out of the maximum of 40. It was becoming more and more obvious to Bela and Marta, that in their still over-serious little trainee they had a future star.

It was a happy family who visited the ancient castle the next morning for a view over the capital of Slovenia and went shopping with Marta. The whole team wanted to buy presents for their families, and Nadia was glad when she found that, after buying something for everybody, she still had enough left to buy the doll she had admired in a tourist shop. Glamorous in her gaily coloured national costume, the Slovenian girl was the perfect momento – Marta agreed – to celebrate Nadia's success.

Putting the doll in the place of honour on her bedroom table, Nadia determined to make her the first of an international family, to

Nadia the public performer

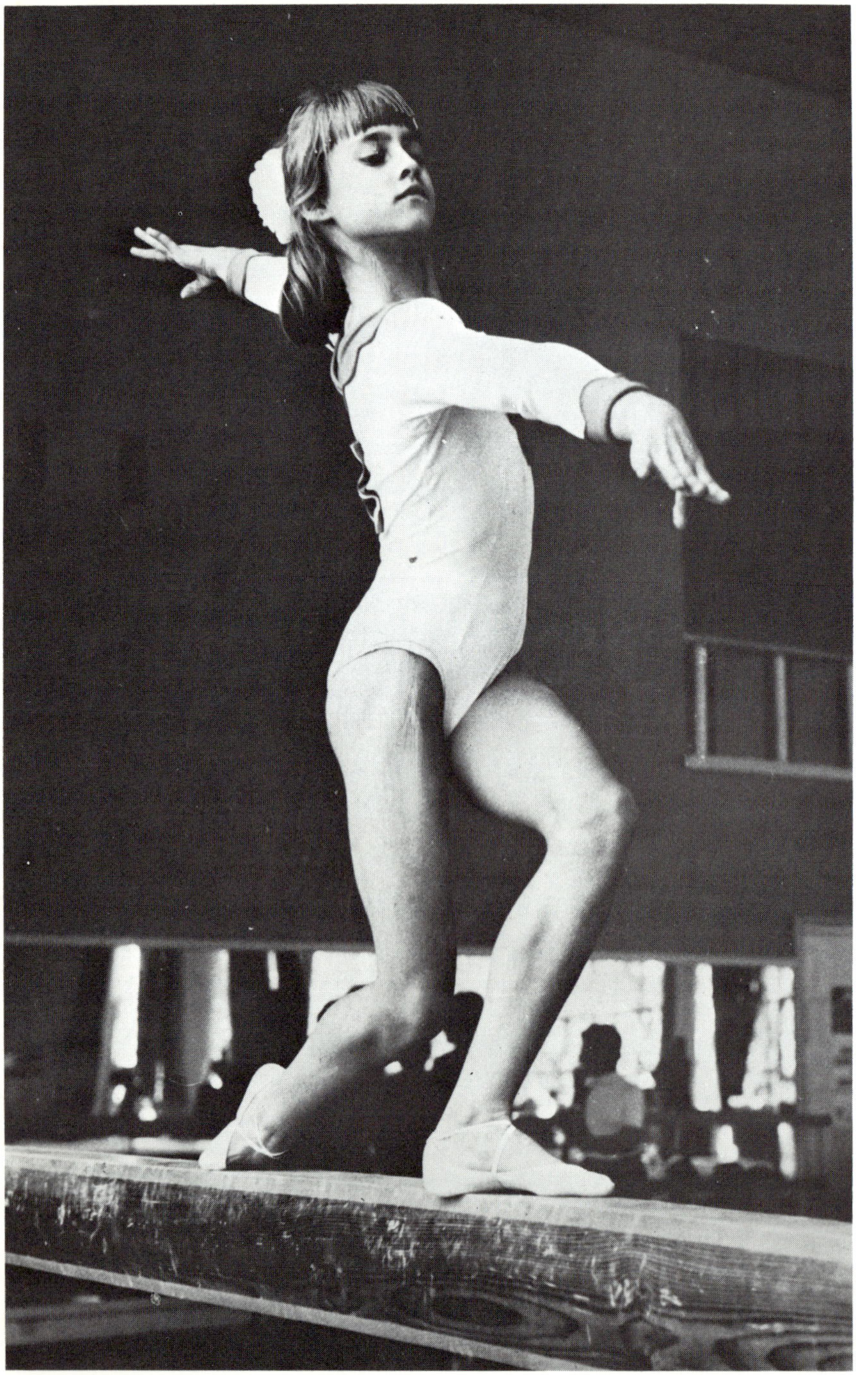

Towards competition standard

which she would add with her every trip abroad. She was delighted when Teodora was intrigued with the idea on her return from the holidays and wanted to found a family of her own. It made a new form of competition between them. Teodora was anxious at last to be selected for the necessary contests with other countries.

However, unknown to both of them, Bela had included Nadia in a team of six which he was to take to a major national contest at his home town of Cluj. This was just twenty-one days after her tenth birthday. It was to give her a head start, with the prospect of many important contests ahead.

This time it was not just presents that their fascinating little daughter was to take home to her astonished but infinitely proud parents, but the five gold medals that Gheorghe placed for everyone to see beside the shining silver cup that accompanied them, the Fourth Category Trophy of the Romanian National Federation.

The young stylist, with her coach

39

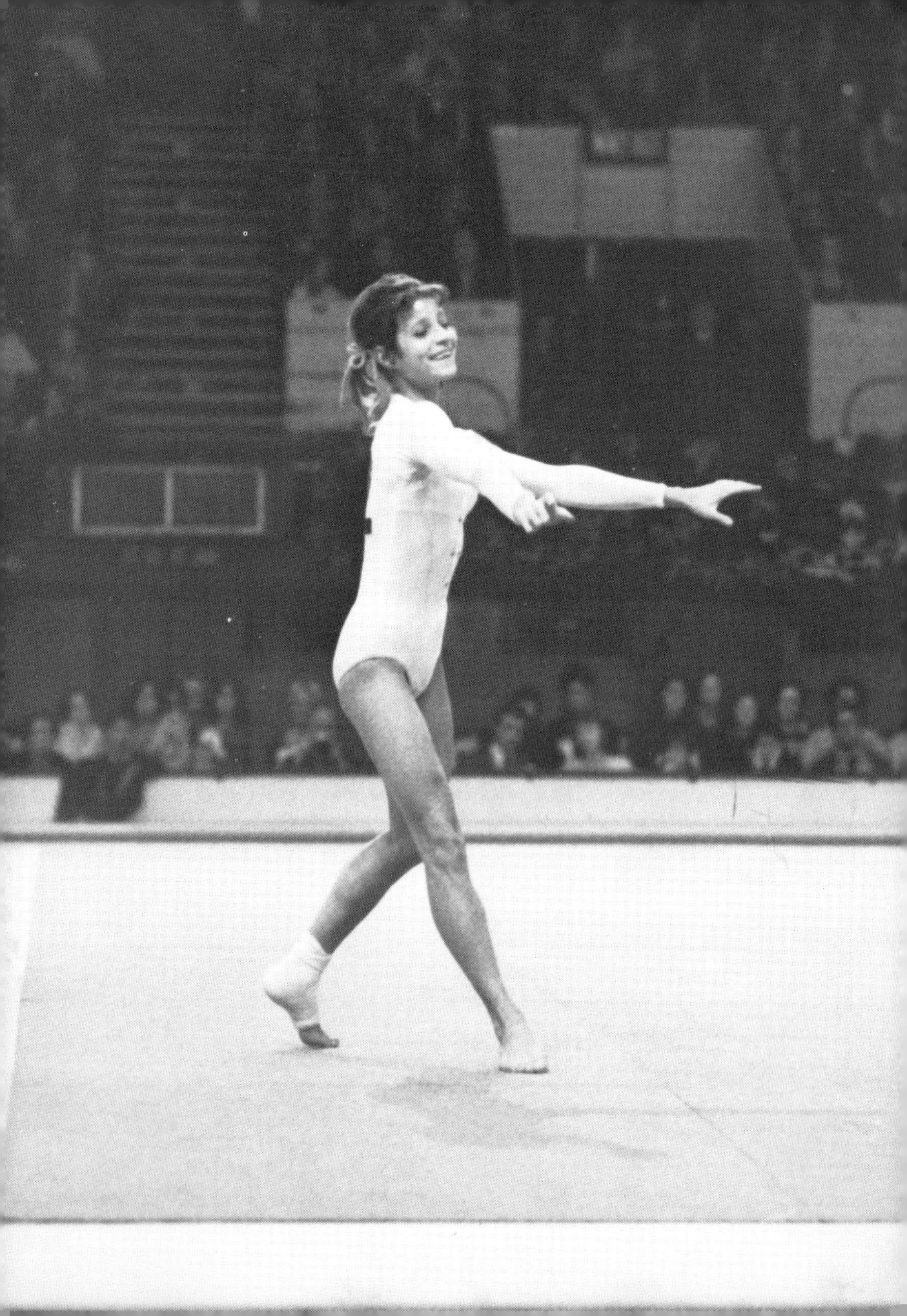

4 THE CHALLENGE OF OLGA KORBUT

The Olympic year of 1972 had athletes from all over the world looking towards the Games that were to open in Munich in late August. Reports were coming from everywhere of the fine new stadium, which, with its fantastic roof, had been constructed upon the site of a war-time aerodrome, the dump for hundreds of thousands of tons of bomb-damage rubble. There were many stories of the ingenuity that had transformed a scene of devastation into the tranquillity of a park green with linden trees transplanted from the surrounding countryside – a place that was to offer peace and beauty and companionship to men of all colours, creeds and nationalities, who were to meet in friendly combat in the true spirit of the Olympic tradition. Happy in his role of host, the warm-hearted, youth-loving Willi Daume, President of the Olympic Committee for Germany, was insisting that there should be nothing political – no military bands or marching – but only a gay parading of the competitors on opening day, to the music of their native folklore.

Knowing little or nothing of the Games, Nadia was curious about them. She became more and more excited at what she heard and discussed it all with Teodora.

It wasn't the preparations that inspired them – although these were impressive – nor even the Olympic ideal, about which they were, as yet, rather vague, but the chance of one day winning a medal for their country – as Atanasia Ionescu had done in Rome, at a contest which was said to be the highest goal of all. Listening avidly to everything that was said of the Olympics, they learned that the next ones would be four years away. Could they be good enough by that time? They decided to ask Mrs Mili. She, it had been proudly said, was to be a Master Judge.

Olga Korbut

The challenge of Olga Korbut

Mrs Mili listened carefully, as they knew she would. She smiled:

'And so you are aiming for the Olympics?' she said slowly. 'And why not?' she added with her quick smile. 'It's always good to aim high. And to tell you a secret, it's what we are hoping for for you. But you must understand, my dears, that there's a long, long way to go. You would first have to prove yourselves to be among the best gymnasts in the world. There is a contest called the pre-Olympics at which you would have to be considered. It's no easy thing, I can tell you, and it could mean years and years of much harder work than you can imagine.'

'How many?' Nadia asked abruptly.

Mrs Mili shrugged. 'That depends, Nadia. Now, let me see. You are just ten years old and in four years from now you will still be only 14.'

'But I will be 15,' Teodora said quickly.

'Yes, but you would still be very young – and do you suppose that you could be better than Nadia?'

'Sometimes I am,' Teodora said defensively.

The two girls looked at each other.

'These things cannot be predicted,' Mrs Mili told them. 'All that you can do is to work steadily and know that we'll be watching you and helping all the way. But you can't hurry things, you know. You just have to go step by step.'

For the next few weeks it was just a case of concentrating on routine exercises and disciplines – measuring and chalking positions on the beam and repeating the same thing over and over until the smallest fault had been eliminated. Bela and Marta were needing to give special attention to a second junior team which Bela had now formed and which he had entered for various contests. It included the graceful Iuliana Marcu, Ana Barcan and the amusing but clever little Luminita Milea, and was doing well.

A lovely surprise at this time for Teodora was the news that everything had been settled at last for her mother to join her in Gheorghiu-Dej. The two-roomed flat which they would occupy in a block not too far from the Comanecis had already been assigned to them, and Emilia would be bringing the treasures that her young daughter had had to leave behind but she was now longing to show to Nadia. It had been fun living in the hostel, Teodora said, but it could never be the same as being in your own home, where you could help with the shopping and cook and sew. Now Nadia would be able to come in and out just as she herself had done at the Comanecis.

Mrs Mili

'How many?' Nadia ponders on an Olympic future.

Nadia was equally glad for her, and Stefania had taken a cutting from the plant which grew around their sitting-room, all ready for her to take to grow around their own wall when Emilia arrived.

It was on 27 May that year that the first international contest between Romania and Bulgaria took place – this time at Gheorghiu-Dej. The result was close, with the points of the home team – Nadia, Mariana, Viorica, Constanta and Liliana Branisteanu – totalling 185 against the visiting team's 185.80. Nadia won the asymmetrical bars and floor disciplines, and Mariana Cojanu was second on the beam.

Teodora with her mother

The challenge of Olga Korbut

The challenge of Olga Korbut

In June they went to Timişoara, where Bela was disappointed that they should be beaten by a superior German team. Only Nadia managed to achieve a third total. But Mili Simionescu thought they had done well for nine- and ten-year-olds, and the experience in itself was valuable.

Bela's disappointment was not so easily assuaged. To his mind the far greater experience was to be the major international contest to be held in Sofia, in Bulgaria, at the end of July. The aim was to find the Olympic Hopes of the future, and there were to be contestants from East Germany, Hungary, Czechoslovakia and the practically unbeatable USSR. He wasn't hopeful for the girls' chances, but he thought it would be good to show them what they were up against. Setting out with Marta and his team of four – Nadia, Mariana, Georgeta and Liliana – he had warned them that they would be competing against accepted internationalists – Biciukina, Ostanina, Metveschi, Shann and Nelli Kim.

Happy with the travelling which took them into yet another country, none of them had seemed over-worried, and it was Marta who was anxious at the thought of their disappointment, as she looked towards them sitting demurely in their places near the podium. Turning away from them, she glanced too at Bela as he stood rubbing the bars with magnesia for their small, ungloved hands. Was it her imagination that he looked sterner even than usual? Could it be that he was regretting the impulse of subjecting his comparatively untried team to an ordeal which was likely to leave them disappointed? He smiled as he passed them to return to his seat, and she thought he looked relieved at the lack of concern in their faces.

With the standard higher even than usual, the result was a surprise such as few of the coaches who were there are likely to forget. For, with a near-perfect performance on the bars and the beam and the attainment of a top total, Nadia mounted the dais to receive three gold medals – and a silver for good measure. It was a sensation – and, for Bela and Marta, an outcome that seemed to justify their wildest dreams! What were they going to do with this wonder child, they were being asked. At ten-and-a-half, it was unbelievable! How did her coaches see her future?

Only Nadia herself sat frowning a little, dismayed at the notice she was attracting. For, while she was glad to have done so well and to have pleased Marta and Bela, it was over now and she hated people crowding round and making a fuss. Essentially a shy and reserved child, she had yet to appreciate the price of fame.

The challenge of Olga Korbut

The rest of the girls had also done better than Bela had anticipated, and the team was placed fourth. But for the Karolys history had been made with Nadia's first great international win. . . .

It was fun going back to the hotel where the teams were staying. At meal times the dining-room was gay with noisy chatter in five languages. Nadia, though younger, was happy and at ease with the other girls, among whom there was a natural sense of camaraderie. Apart from the cheer that went up as the little champion entered, and the occasional nonchalant congratulations, nobody now fussed over her. She had beaten them this time, but no one was downcast; their turn would come. With the tension over, the coaches conferred at their separate table and were no longer so mindful of their charges. The conversation was a happy cacophony of exclamations and argument, and a reasonable understanding was achieved in the international language of the gym.

It was fun, too, to go shopping once again in a new country, and with the Bulgarian money that Bela had exchanged in a kiosk Nadia chose presents for her parents, her grandmother, and her brother Adrian.

Then there was the final excitement of the journey home with the medals that were to be her special gift to Stefania and Gheorghe. Both were there as she burst into the flat with the gold and silver trophies hanging from their ribbons. Bela and Marta were behind her, anxious to tell of her triumph. But now, waiting only for her mother to pass the medals to her father – who remarked that with the ever-increasing number they were going to need a glass-fronted cabinet to display them in – Nadia had lost interest and begged to be allowed to find Teodora for a game of tennis. It was to be like this with all her medals. Almost as soon as they were placed about her neck, they were to be disregarded by her as yesterday's achievement – holding little interest for her except as momentos of countries she had visited. Always her restless mind would be jumping ahead to the next step – to a new difficulty to overcome. It is no mock-modesty that renders her indifferent to her accomplishments and makes her forever strive for what is beyond her reach. Nor is it due to conceit that she actively dislikes flattery or limelight. She shrinks from it. With her considerable intelligence, Nadia might have been better suited to the career of a scientist, and found an outlet for her remarkable dedication and concentration in the privacy of a laboratory. . . .

With the summer holiday once again before them, Gheorghe and Stefania took the children this year to Mangalia, the most southerly of

The challenge of Olga Korbut

Romania's seaside resorts. Its modernity contrasts strangely with the remains of the ancient Greek city that flourished on the site in the sixth century BC, and with the oriental mosque built by the Turks at a much later date: but such things were of little interest to the six-year-old Adrian, who was now a keen participant in the games of football on the wide beach, while, for Nadia, the main attraction was always to be the sea and the swimming, which she looks upon as her second sport.

A row of young swimmers, with Nadia on the right

The Ungureanus were already installed in their new flat in Gheorghiu-Dej, and the end of the holidays saw Nadia and Teodora anxiously awaiting for the start of the Munich Olympics on 26 August. The Romanian contingent had left a week or so earlier – the athletes, oarsmen, wrestlers, gymnasts and the many others who, from all parts of the country, had been given a great send-off.

Those watching the Opening Day on television could hardly fail to be impressed with the joy and spirit of unity that prevailed, as the finest of the world's youth sang the Olympic hymn in unison and stood to watch the raising of the flag, the release of the doves, the arrival of the flame to ignite the Olympic Fire, and, last but not least, the taking of the oath. For Willi Daume, who had taken part in the Games of '36, and who now sought, in different times, to bring back something of the true Olympic spirit, the sincerity and the simplicity of the scene before him must have been one of the great moments of his life.

For Nadia and Teodora, though they were enthralled with the

thought that they too might one day be a part of it all, it was the women's gymnastics due to start the day after in the fine new Sports Hall in the Olympic Park that was all-important. But they listened to it all. For the five days from 27 August to 1 September, they were scarcely away from the radio. The Romanian team having won a third place in Rome in 1960 – which had given Atanasia her bronze medal – they were hoping against hope that the new team would avenge the drop to sixth place in Tokyo in 1964. Too young, however, as yet for even their talk with Mrs Mili to have made them aware that, with the increase of interest in the sport, there was to be an enormously strong competition on the podium, their hearts sank as the Romanian team, though clearly worthy contestants, were outclassed by those from other countries, notably the USSR and East Germany. But, disappointed though they were, there was nothing

The challenge of Olga Korbut

grudging in their admiration for a new little Russian star who was captivating the world with her breathtaking 'superior difficulties' and her gamin charm. Just 17 and a mere shrimp of a girl with her height of 4 foot 11 inches, Olga Korbut was already a Grand Master of her sport. She thought nothing of the hitherto unheard-of feat of a back somersault on the beam, and a full twist on and handspring off vault.

Olga Korbut – a back somersault to make hearts leap

The challenge of Olga Korbut

Nadia, recognizing in her a future rival who was clearly going to follow such feats with others equally spectacular, so as to win bonus points, could not wait to try them out and to do a little improving on them herself. Olga, indeed, created a stir that was to earn her a following throughout the world. She had an easy win on both the beam and the floor, and tied with Erika Zuchold of East Germany for second place on the asymmetrical bars. She was to return to her home in Grodno, near the Polish border, with three gold medals and a silver. The USSR were the overall winners, followed closely by East Germany – for whom Karin Janz had won both the bars and the vault. Hungary, America, Czechoslovakia and Romania came third, fourth, fifth and sixth respectively, leaving everyone else way behind.

Nadia, and everyone in the Gimnastica, were eagerly awaiting the return of Mrs Mili to tell them all about it. Knowing that she was a great patriot, Nadia and Teodora were expecting her to be very disappointed, not fully understanding that as a dedicated gymnast she was thrilled with the progress that was being made in the art that meant so much to her, and that with the complete success of her concept of the Gimnastica at Gheorghiu-Dej, her heart was filled with delight at all it promised for the future.

With the end of the gymnastics and the start of a new term, it was a good thing perhaps that the children's interest in the Olympics had begun to wane a little before the Munich tragedy occurred. Politically inspired, it was to seem to make a mockery of all that had gone into the Games to make them a symbol of unity in a troubled world.

But for Nadia and Teodora, who were still too young to appreciate the infinite sadness it had brought to those who were better able to understand, it was just another happening that made people shake their heads and talk, but which had no part in their busy lives at school and at the Gimnastica.

5 HOME TOWN TRIUMPHANT

The new autumn term of 1972 seemed to mark the beginning of a great number of contests and exhibitions. The first was against the Socialist Federative Republic of Russia, the largest of the republics that make up the Soviet Union. Held at Gheorghiu-Dej on 29 September, it was the first in Teodora's rather delayed international career. Once again, however, it was to be Nadia's day, with an easy win of a top total over the promising young Russian, Svetlana Grozdova. Teodora's successes – and there were to be many of them – were yet to come.

The next important contest in November was a successful bid for the Junior Romanian Championships in the second category – with Teodora this time making a first appearance on the national scene. One week later the same team of Nadia, Teodora, Liliana, Mariana and Georgeta defeated the Hungarian team in their own capital of Budapest, with Nadia first, Mariana second and Liliana third. Mariana was doing well in every contest, though she had been having trouble with her eyes.

Then, in December, when she was just 11, Nadia once again won the cup at the annual contest in Bucharest for the Romanian National Trophy. There seemed to be no end to her triumphs.

So it was that at the beginning of 1973 – barely eight years after they had decided to pool their resources and seek their champions in the kindergartens – Bela and Marta found that the many teams which they were now able to enter, from the fourth to the master category, in every conceivable major contest brought Gheorghiu-Dej the biggest successes of the country. With each of them congratulating the other on the hard work that had gone into it, they still had to be deeply thankful for the luck that seemed to have followed them all the way. But even as they waited for the baby that Marta was expecting – and

51

At the Sala Floreasca in Bucharest, Nadia, shown here, aged 11, beat Nelli Kim.

that Bela declared was to be the loveliest happening of all – Marta knew that, with the phenomenal successes of Nadia and the promise of Teodora and Georgeta and some of the others, Bela was already looking to the Montreal Olympics of 1976 for the final glory.

It was strange that while Nadia was still putting everything she had into her work and making fine progress, the first few months of the year should see Teodora suddenly defeating her on everything. The two were still inseparable when they were away from the gym, but their rivalry for first place in it was now a talking-point for everyone. Was it the new confidence that Teodora had acquired with her entry into major competition? Or had the need to keep up with Nadia spurred her to an even greater effort? Nobody knew. Whatever the cause, it was all to the good so far as Bela was concerned, for he now saw himself with two all-but-invincible champions.

As if to prove herself, Nadia once again thrilled them all at an international contest at the Floreasca Sala in Bucharest on 14 April when, still only 11, she beat Nelli Kim of Russia and other champions from East Germany, Czechoslovakia and Hungary, winning four gold medals and the individual total. She was now rapidly achieving a reputation as the leading Romanian gymnast, and foreign coaches were fearing her as one of the most formidable opponents in Eastern Europe.

The contest was followed by others in Romania and one, in May, in Poland. In all of them the team did well, with Teodora beginning to show herself as a more than useful member.

In June the girls went to Italy, after an invitation from Mestre to give a special demonstration. It promised to be a highlight for them all, with the special treat of a visit to Venice. Intrigued, now, with tales from Shakespeare, which had replaced her childish passion for fairy stories, Nadia was longing to see the Rialto Bridge of the Merchant of Venice, and the palace on the canal said to have inspired the story of Othello and Desdemona. But there was a disappointment. Teodora was to be left behind. Bela had become irritated by her unpunctuality, and when she had arrived one day five minutes late for a final rehearsal he decided that the time had come to teach her a lesson. It was in vain that the others tried to coax him; once having made up his mind, Bela was obdurate.

The team missed their easy-going, fun-loving companion. But there was a further disappointment to come. When the Italians learnt that they were to see only a bunch of little girls, rather than the more glamorous signorinas they had been expecting, the hall, with its seating capacity for 10,000, had a bare 1,500 for the first performance. Bela was furious. But he was mollified when, after the press notices, the second and third days saw every ticket sold and 'standing room only' notices displayed everywhere.

The most important meeting for the winter term was the Friendship Cup, which was to be held this year in Gera, East

Nadia takes courage from Bela

Germany. Bela took a team of eight – Nadia, Georgeta, Mariana, Gabriela, Liliana, Teodora, Luminita and Iuliana. They had trained hard, but their average age being eleven years and five months, they were up against contestants who were not only older but considerably more experienced. Neither Mili Simionescu nor Bela could be too hopeful, especially with opponents such as Nelli Kim and Nina Dramova from Russia and other strong contenders from Poland and East Germany. It was a delightful surprise therefore when Nadia once again defeated Nelli Kim, winning the asymmetrical bars, the vault and the top total, and Teodora was second on the beam. Three more gold medals and a silver to take home to Gheorghiu-Dej!

After this contest Teodora became the Junior Champion of Romania, and little Luminita Milea, the youngest member of the team, won first place at Pitești. Each of them was now accorded the coveted title of 'Maestra a sportului',* joining Nadia and Anca Grigoras – who had won the outright championship of Romania at the age of 15 in 1972. Bela could be proud of them indeed. Unfortunately Teodora had an accident to her leg soon after, which was to hamper her for some weeks.

*Far above the first category, the title of 'Maestra a sportului' is conferred with an outstanding win in either national or international competition.

55

On 12 November, the day before Teodora's thirteenth birthday, Nadia was 12. They were both of them Pioneers – an organization in which most children are eager to be enrolled into their school units at the age of 9. The aim of the movement is to educate young Romanians in a spirit of patriotism, ethics and equity that will enable them to give of their best to their country. Similar in many ways to Baden-Powell's Scouts and Guides, Pioneers train under an adult Commander. The uniform is attractive – white blouse, bright red tie, buckled belt and navy beret. Most of all, Nadia loved the tie, since red is her favourite colour; she considers it to be lucky for her, just as five is her lucky number.

Nadia was popular with her fellow Pioneers. While still reserved with her teachers, she was adventurous and could be a lot of fun with children and girls of her own age. But with the increasing number of hours she now needed to spend at the gym and with the extra time she had to put in with her school homework to make up for the days she missed with her contests, her few spare hours would invariably find her hurrying off with Teodora for their other sports – cycling, swimming, tennis and, with the coming of the snow, the winter

56

Nadia the Pioneer (left) and girl of all sports

Home town triumphant

sports that they both adored. Neither of their mothers saw much of them in term-time, since it was often easier for them to spend the night at the hostel, if they were busy practising and likely to be leaving early in the morning.

Their lives were becoming busier all the time, but they wouldn't have changed them for the world. Like the other girls in the team, they were now so used to travelling that they thought little of it. Young as they were, they were already clever at packing, knowing exactly what they would need and always having such things as sewing materials handy in case of accidents. Mrs Mili considers them to be amazingly resourceful, and she laughs as she tells of how they often offer to help with her packing in addition to their own. She loves travelling with them.

The first interesting contest of 1974 was against the Americans, who came to Gheorghiu-Dej from Denver, Colorado. With a team from Poland making it a three-cornered battle, the Gheorghiu-Dej team was victorious. Nadia won the individual total and the other girls did well too, especially Luminita. The American coach, Rod Hill, singled Nadia out as 'the finest junior gymnast I have ever seen'.

Next they went off on an exciting trip to Korea – Nadia, Teodora, Georgeta, Luminita, Gabriela, Iuliana Marcu and Mariana Cojanu. It was for the Phenian Tour of Friendship and the most noteworthy contest of the year. It was all the more disappointing that a minor injury should occur to handicap Nadia from the outset. Struggling valiantly with the vault, the asymmetrical bars and the beam, she had to retire for the floor. Nevertheless the honours went once again to Gheorghiu-Dej, when Teodora took gold medals for both the beam and bars, and Mariana won a bronze.

That summer Bela took the team to the sea for a special training period. Every child at the Gimnastica is given constant medical care, and the resident doctor, Gheorghe Lazar, was watching these young adolescents with an eagle eye for their general well-being. He liked them to work in the open air whenever possible, and it was becoming a regular thing for Bela and Marta to seize every opportunity that offered between contests for a trip to the mountains or to the '2 Mai' camp at Mangalia. It will be remembered that while Bela and Marta are the top trainers at Gheorghiu-Dej, there are many others, including especially Florin and Florica Dobre, who are responsible for the training of the girls assigned to them. In this way the Gimnastica functions as usual during the Karolys' absence.

In October Bela took Nadia and Teodora to France for an

The team relaxes on the beam, with a Karoly on either end.

important demonstration and contest in which there were a large number of gymnasts of different ages. Because of their youth, Nadia and Teodora were to perform in a small hall in the suburbs of the capital. Bela objected and insisted that they should be allowed to compete with the older contestants in a large hall in the centre of Paris. This marked the first occasion when Nadia was to meet the famous Ludmila Tourischeva. She became an overnight sensation when she defeated the top Russian star. She was pleased with her success, but wasn't going to allow it to make her overconfident. She had yet to meet Olga Korbut who, she considered, would present the greatest challenge of them all. . . .

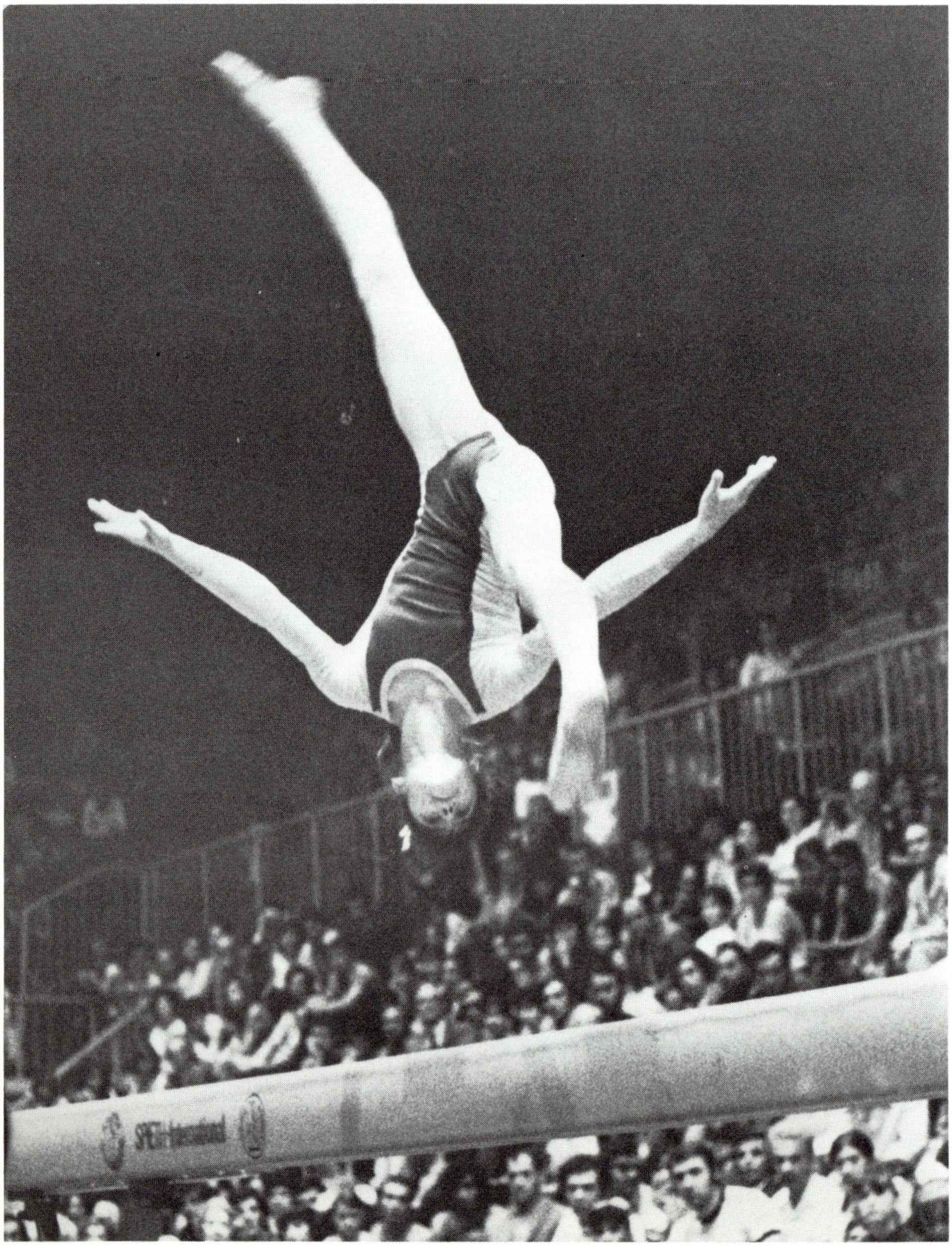

6   EUROPEAN CHAMPION

With the dawning of 1975, anyone who had been in the precincts of the Sports Club on the first day of the spring term would surely have seen the inseparables, Nadia and Teodora, striding along the path that leads to the Gimnastica. Teodora would have been chatting away as usual and Nadia turning her head to interject a dry remark which, accompanied by the derisive, impish smile that is characteristic of her, comes like a flash of sunshine to banish the seriousness of her expression. It was three years now since their naïve little talk with Mrs Mili concerning the Montreal Olympics – three years during which the all but unbelievable progress they had made had convinced Bela that they could hold their own against the toughest opposition. Young as they would be at 14 and 15 in 1976, Bela had decided that they were to go to the pre-Olympics in the coming July.

His decision came as no surprise to Mili Simionescu, who shared his delight and enthusiasm and took it for granted that they would go. Nor was it a surprise to the girls themselves. They were no longer children but master gymnasts. They were well aware of their capabilities, and also of those of their prospective rivals, whom they had already met in international contest. Appreciating the distance that still had to be run in the seventeen months that lay ahead, they regarded it as a challenge after their own hearts, as they set out with zest and determination, together with Georgeta Gabor, Mariana Constantin and Marilena Neacsu – and others who would be considered at Bacău later in the year.

With such an aim in view, everyone had a part to play in the attainment of a world victory for their beloved Romania: Bela and Marta, as the superb trainers whose expertise could lead to perfection; Poszar with his brilliant imagination and verve; Stabişevschi, whose

European champion

music was an inspiration; and the girls who trusted and depended upon them all. It was a happy relationship that made for success.

For Nadia, the first step was to represent Romania in the Champions All contest in England at Wembley, in April, organized by the *Daily Mirror*. Countries had been invited to send two champions, one of either sex, to compete for a special trophy. The contest was to be held annually and promised to be an event for which seats would need to be booked months in advance by anyone eager to see the world's top gymnasts in action. That Nadia was to be something of a surprise to the organizers is clearly shown in the following paragraph written by Frank Taylor, the *Mirror*'s sportswriter:*

Nadia's sequence to the Straddle shows a strong thrust from her wrists to her toes.

* See the *Daily Mirror Comaneci Story*, by Frank Taylor.

I was sitting in my office on Friday, April 14th, the day before the first ever Champions All Tournament, when the telephone rang. It was Tony Murdoch, the development officer of the British Amateur Gymnastic Association, who said: 'You had better get down to Wembley as quick as you can, with a photographer. There is a little Romanian girl here called Nadia Comaneci who is spinning around the asymmetrical bars like a catherine wheel. I've never seen anything like it. She's going to be a sensation if she performs like this in the real competition tomorrow. I can't see how she can lose.'

Twelve countries competed, including the Soviet Union, East and West Germany, and Hungary. Avril Lennox represented Great Britain. Nadia won, although she had barely recovered from a bout of flu. Mrs Mili, who had come with her, was over the moon with delight. . . .

63

At the Champions All contest in London, April 1975, Nadia delights her audience with a backward Tinsica . . . and goes on to win.

64

The new champion photographed with Avril Lennox of Great Britain

European champion

But the most ambitious venture of all was the European Championship, which was to be held in Skein, in Norway. Attracting a world press coverage, countries everywhere were looking to their best gymnasts to bring home the coveted trophy. Without much hope, Romania was sending Alina Goreac, who was 22, and had trained with considerable success under Nicolae Cavaci at the Dinamo Club in Bucharest. To her very considerable number of medals and trophies Alina had added in 1974 the title of Absolute Balkan Woman Champion. Nadia was to go along too. There was perhaps a latent hope in Bela's mind that with her composure and determination she could put herself somewhere in the running, but neither he nor Mrs Mili were allowing themselves to be optimistic. And so they set off – Nicolae Cavaci and Bela, the two coaches, Mili Simionescu, Stabişevschi and the two girls. Nadia was silent in the plane, and thinking that she looked small and defenceless Mili's heart went out to her.

'Are you scared, Nadia?' she asked.

'No,' the little girl said simply.

'Are you thinking that the others are going to be better than you?'

'No.'

'Not Tourischeva?'

'No.'

'Nor Nelli Kim?'

'No. The only one that can scare me is Teodora.'

The newspapers Bela brought into the hotel that evening were full of the next day's contest. Both sportswriters and readers were forecasting the results. Some favoured Zinche, many Tourischeva or Kim; these three seemed to be the top favourites. Alina was mentioned as a long shot. Nadia's name did not appear anywhere.

The arena was packed throughout the days of the contest, and there was a greater tension than usual in the silence that fell as each competitor mounted the podium. Sitting in the audience with Cavaci, Bela was expressionless when it came to Nadia's turn. Thinking back, he will say that he was seeing again the grave stare that had greeted his final injunction to her: 'Now, Nadia, here's your chance to show the whole world what you can do.'

Swinging into a magnificent performance on the asymmetrical bars, in which she was including an element of daring which they had perfected together, Nadia executed her famous Radochla with an ease that led the Soviet coach, Rastorsky, to exclaim: 'The girl has nerves of steel! . . . She amazes me!'

66 *The Comaneci Radochla and* OVERLEAF
an incredible leap from the floor.

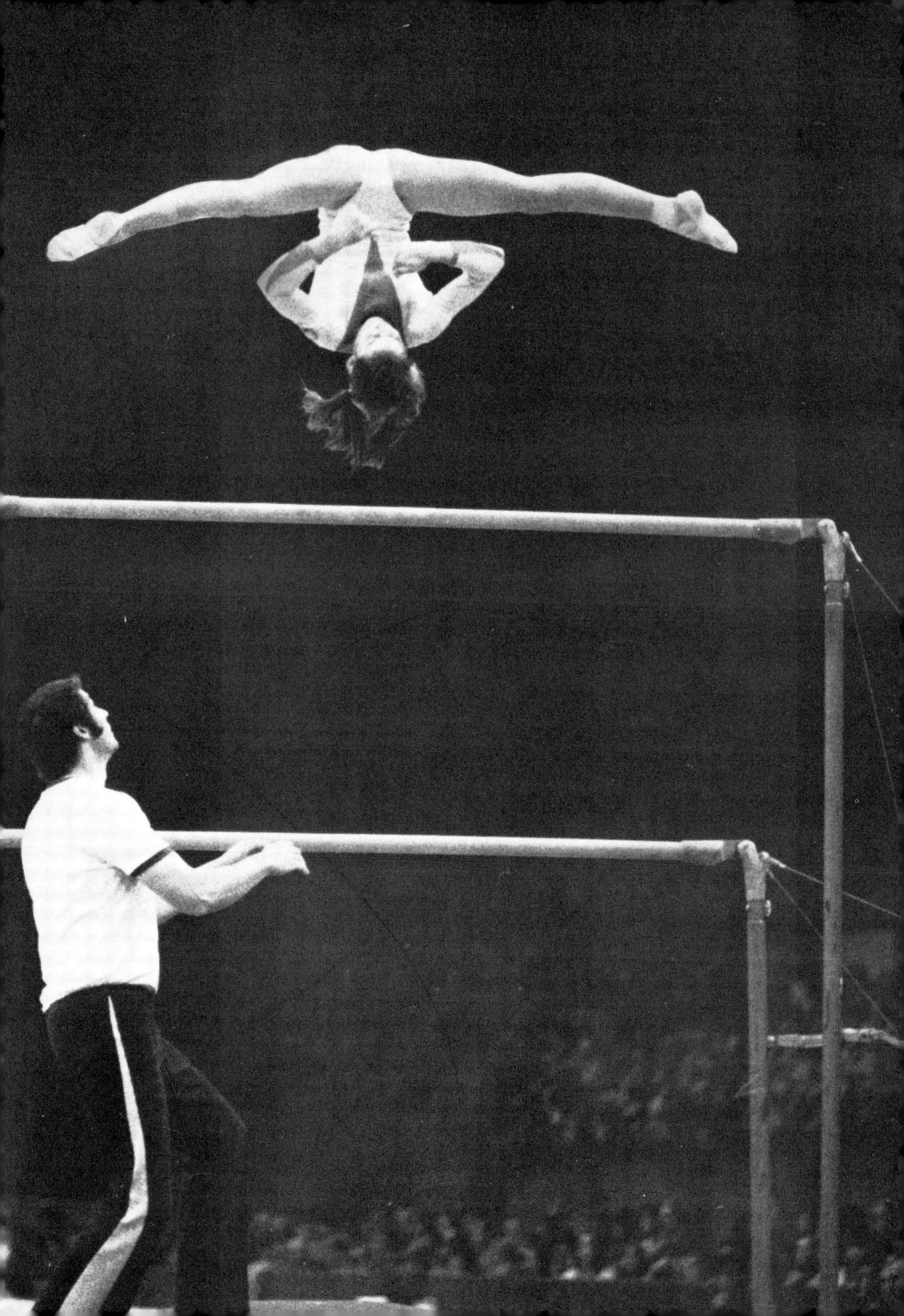

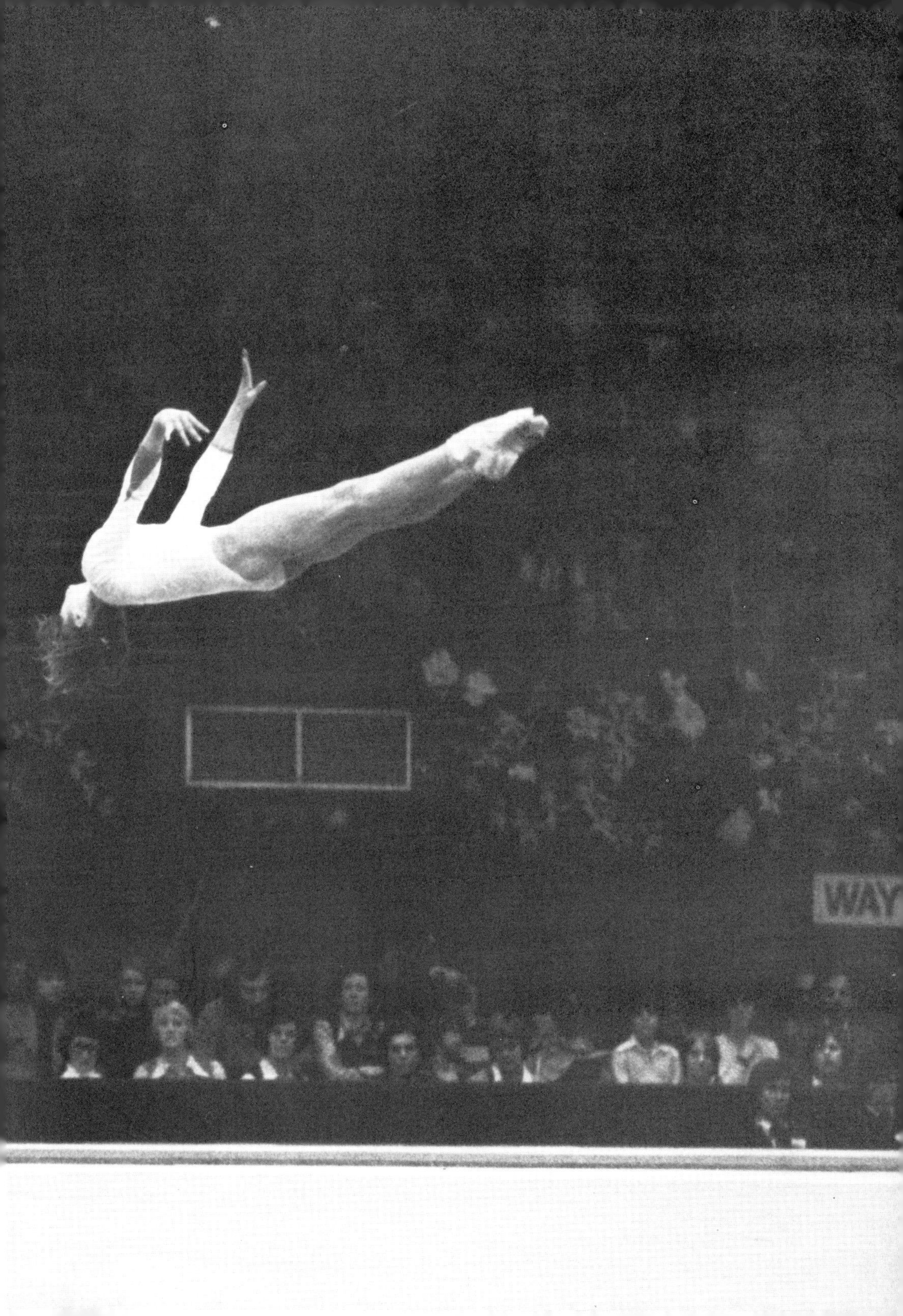
WAY

European champion

The judges awarded her 9.90 and she went on to give a Tsukahara vault that was said by many to be the finest they had ever seen.

Far away in Romania, her countrymen were following her exploits and laughing and crying in turns, as each of her successive wins of four gold medals and a silver were acknowledged with the playing of their national anthem.

Tsukahara piked vault

The new European Champion returns triumphant from Norway, and finds herself a star. Admiring youngsters crowd around to see her trophies.

European champion

Life from then on was a blur for Nadia, as she stood with the trophy held high above her head, while the photographers' lights flashed about her and people everywhere were asking questions. She was happy – happy for Mrs Mili, happy for Bela, happy, most of all, for Romania! It was a beautiful trophy, the best yet, and her mother and father were going to be delighted.

Mobbed by the press and the crowd until the very last minute, Nadia returned in triumph to Bucharest, to be greeted at the airport by the President of the National Council of Physical Education and Sport, who took the tiny champion into his arms and kissed her. Then came the drive through the capital with the crowds showering her with flowers.

It was her first great win for her country. There could have been nothing to mar her joy, save for the natural reluctance of an essentially shy and reserved young patriot to be thrust into the limelight of a growing fame.

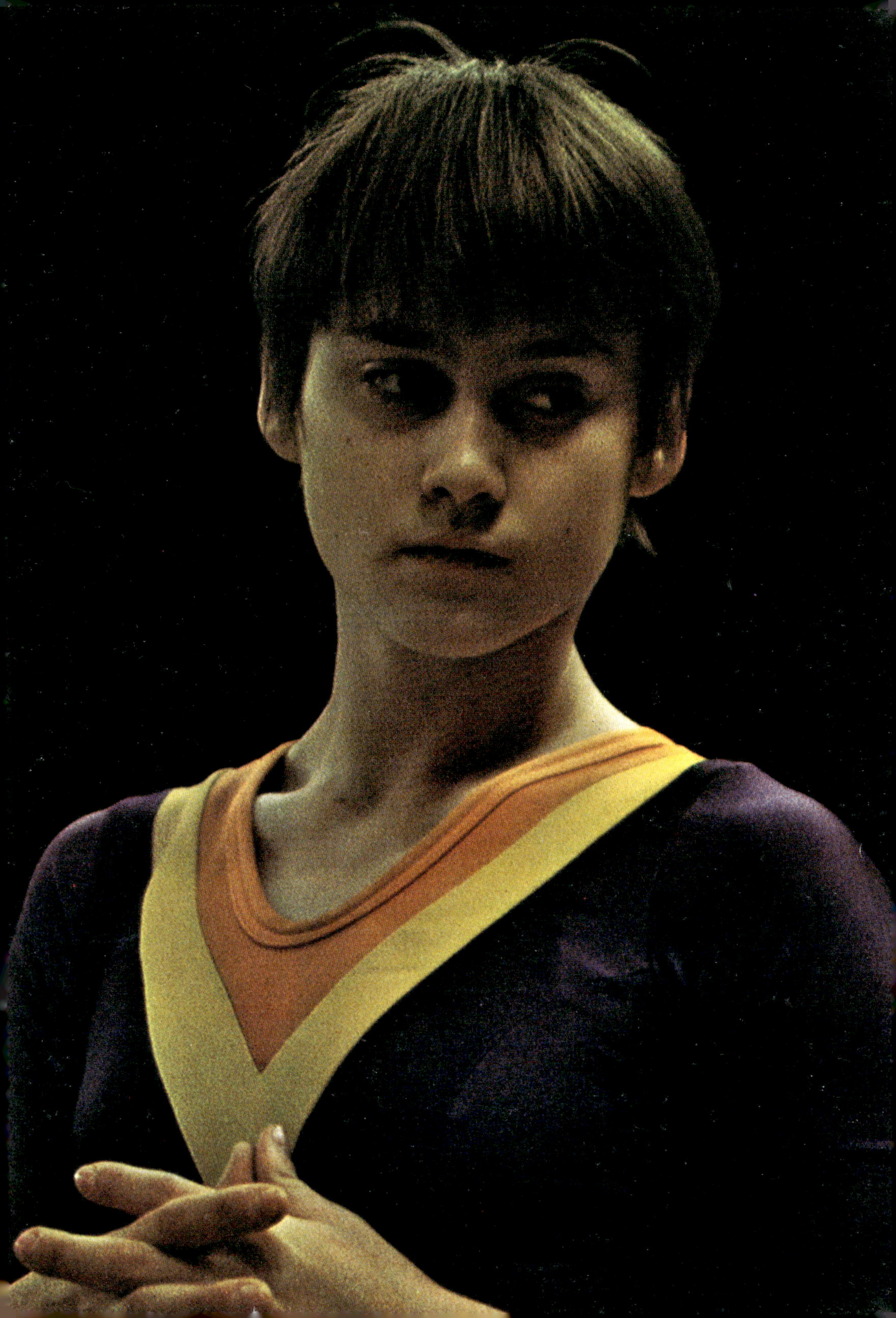

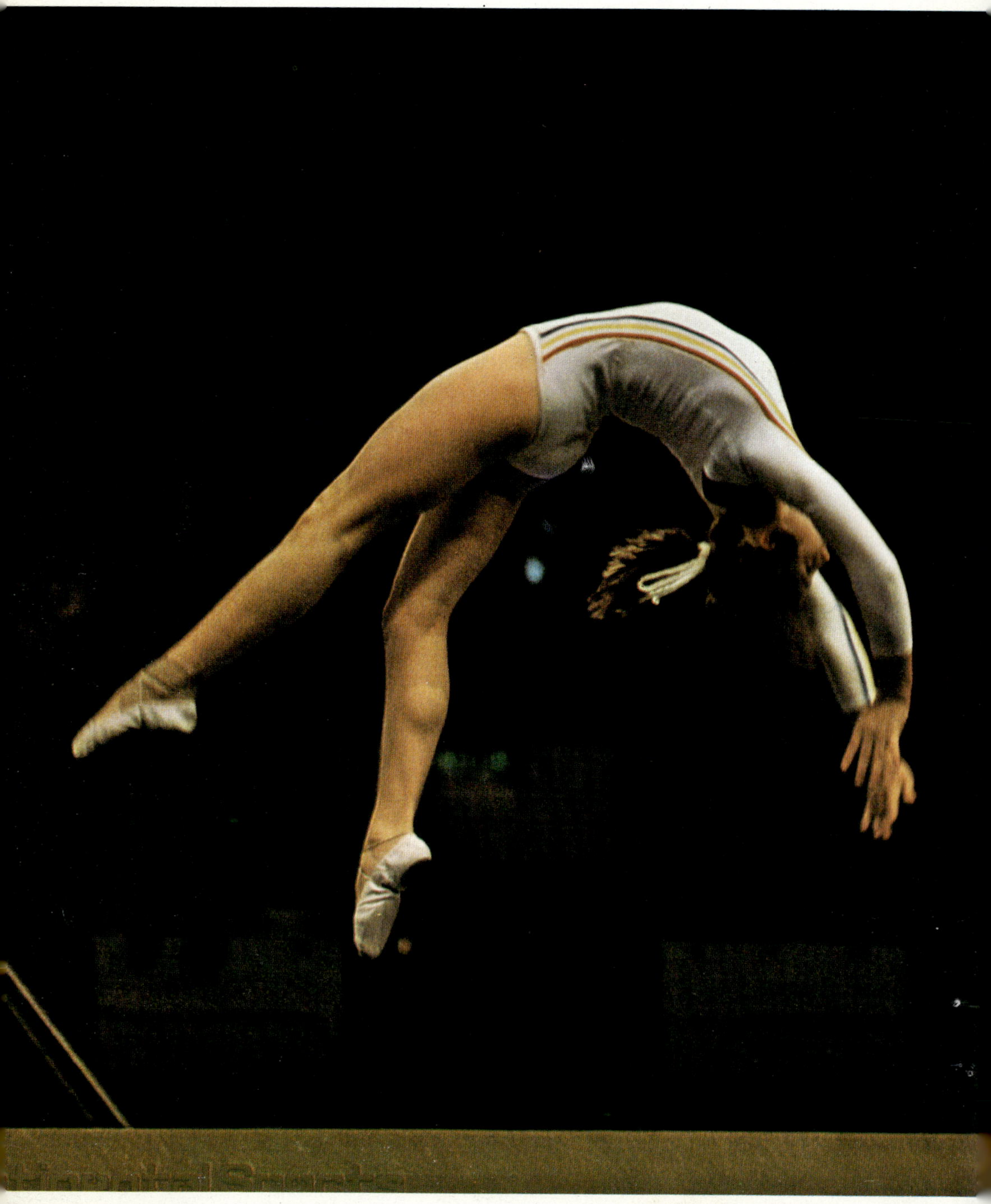

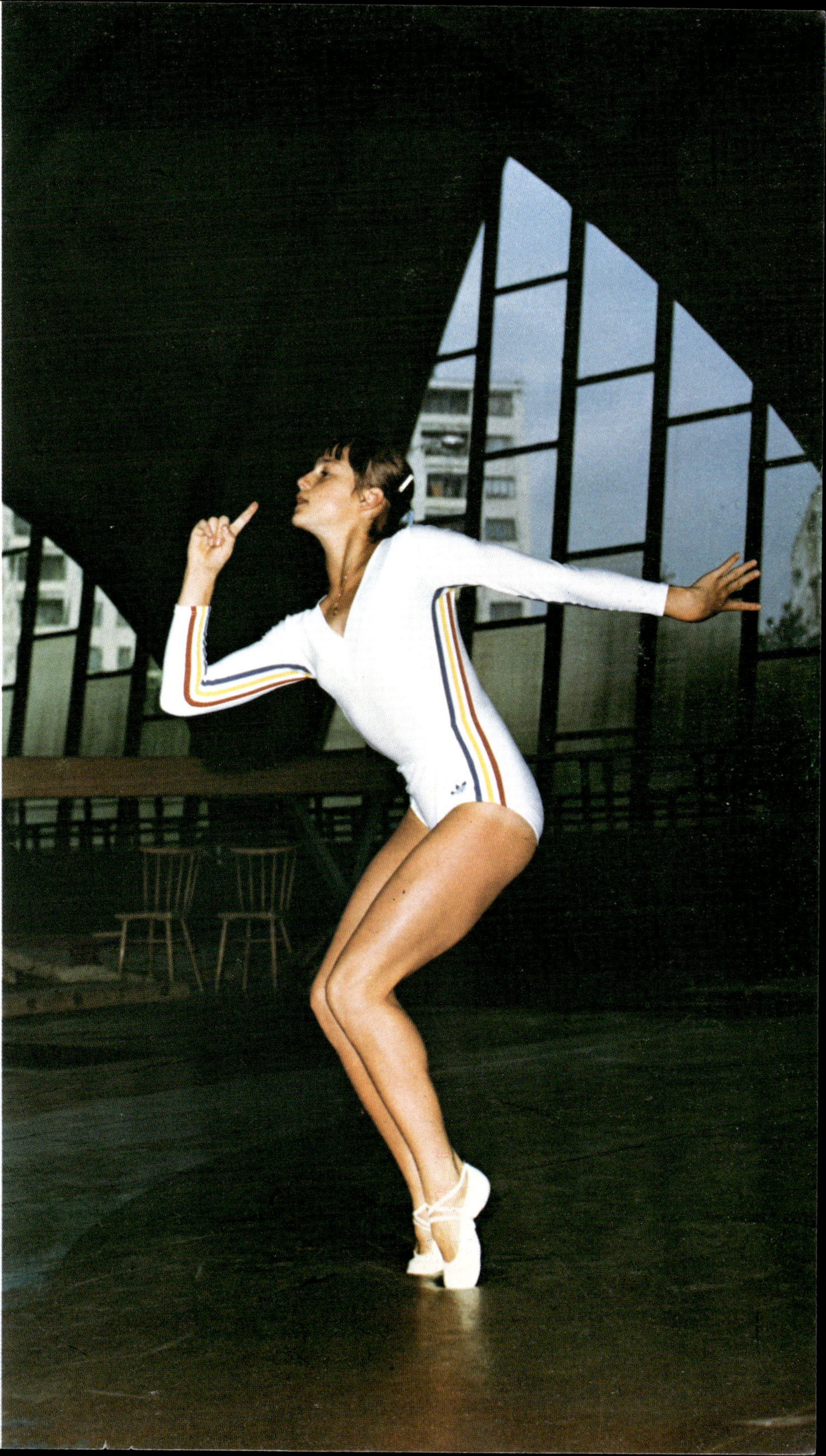

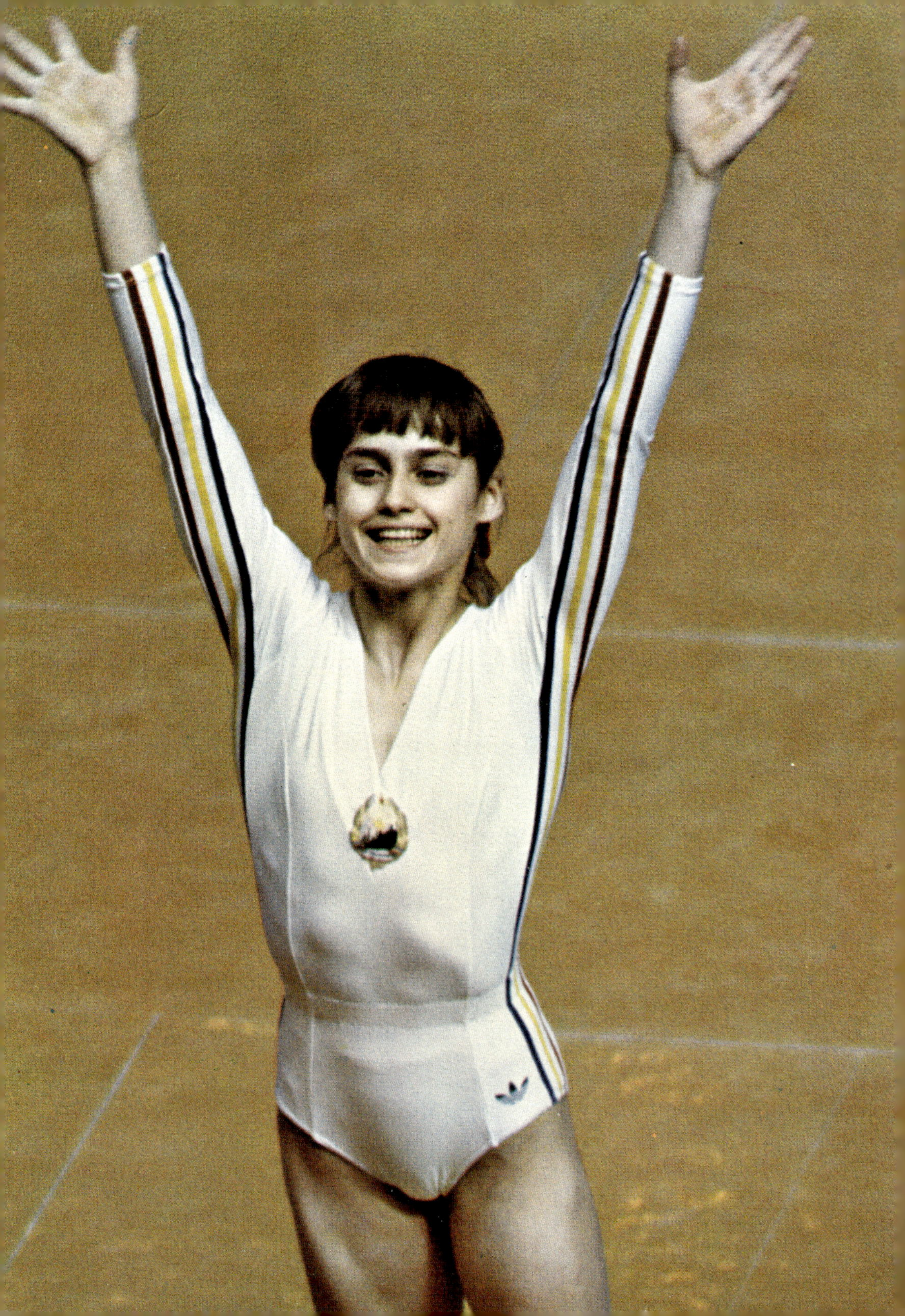

7 THE FIRST EVER 'PERFECT 10'

It was only with her return to Gheorghiu-Dej that Nadia was fully to appreciate the joy that her success had brought to the country and to her own town in particular. The people came hurrying to greet her, with the young Pioneers carrying a banner announcing:

BRAVO NADIA!
Tot inainte!*

In her own element now – among those whom she knew and in the place that means more to her than anywhere else in the world – she could share their pride and delight as the trophy, and her newest medals, were passed around for all to see.

Once again she was besieged with questions. But this time they were not from reporters running beside her with cameras. And they were in her own language. What was it like? Had she been nervous when waiting for her turn? Had she thought that she could win?

Yes, was her answer to the last. But there was no trace of conceit. She wouldn't have been able to explain it to them. But deep in her heart she knew that after working with Bela for twenty-four hours a week,† his keen eye assessing her at all times, she now had won his final approval and had reached the standard of excellence at which he was aiming. Added to which was the self-discipline that armed her against shyness and resulting nerves, and prevented her, as she mounted the steps to the podium, from being conscious of anything except the familiarity of the scene that lay before her. Going through her disciplines, one after the other, with her slim supple body

---

* Bravo Nadia! – once again!
† Nadia trains at the Gimnastica for four hours and goes to school for another five every day but Sunday. Work at either place starts at 8 o'clock in the morning.

automatically responding to the meticulous attention to detail that her quick brain demanded of it, she could be totally free of any emotional strain that might have marred her performance and know that the best she could do would at least be as good as yesterday's and probably better.

This was an admirable philosophy for the strong character that Nadia had proved herself to be since childhood. Still very young, and happiest in a simple, organized life with the challenge of her contests as highlights, she has an unsmiling manner which can seem aloof to strangers and can give a false impression. Her headmistress, Mrs Maria Pop, says that she is a quiet, book-loving and unassuming girl who, while she can be as full of laughter and fun as any of her companions, lives in a world of her own.

Comaneci movement on the beam. A backward walk-over and two flick-flacs off one leg.

Nadia's astonishing win at Skein had now given her a reputation in countries far beyond the boundaries of Eastern Europe and excited a world interest in what she was likely to accomplish at the pre-Olympics in July. Bela was concentrating on achieving new and even more spectacular 'difficulties' which could bring bonus points. None of these, however, were to be included in her programme until he could be confident that she had acquired an ease and control over them to make them safe. Never happier than when striving for what was out of reach, Nadia would set about mastering the new feats with a complete absorption, as she analysed their holds and timing and other technical problems, until Bela would call a halt and send her off to rest.

A free cartwheel and flick-flac off one leg. Drawings by Atanasia Ionescu-Albu, Romanian Olympic coach.

The first ever 'Perfect 10'

Teodora, still a close second to her, was also doing well, and everyone concerned was optimistic of their chances. There was a growing number of younger gymnasts – as many as 48 aspirants at the qualifying contest. The standard was higher than it had ever been. Once again Nadia was to top the list by winning the asymmetrical bars and the all-round title, while Teodora was second on the beam, third on the floor and third, also, behind her compatriot and Nelli Kim, in the all-round. After an enthusiastic press, world promotors who had been anticipating a major battle at the '76 Olympics between the popular little Olga Korbut and Comaneci, the new star, were thinking again in the light of Kim's three individual wins of the beam, vault and floor.

Returning happily enough from Canada with two gold and three silver medals, the girls celebrated by buying themselves the Eskimo dolls that were to add to their international collection. Nadia's was still the larger family, but Teodora was happy at the prospect of catching up a little when it was decided that, with Nadia left behind this time, she and Georgeta Gabor were to fly to an international contest in Tokyo at the end of August.

Bela with his prize-winning gymnasts. From the left: Iuliana Marcu, Teodora Ungureanu, Nadia Comaneci, Calina Hosu and, in front, Georgeta Gabor and Luminita Milea. On the right, a team photo with Mariana Constantin, Marilena Neacsu, Teodora, Nadia, Iuliana and Luminita.

The first ever 'Perfect 10'

Japan has produced some of the greatest gymnasts in the world (providing the origin of Nadia's famous 'Tsukahara vault'), but it is only in recent years that Japanese women have been permitted to participate. With the new and keen interest that has already brought a number of them to Olympic standard, it can only be a question of time before they prove as formidable as their men before them.

This was not to be their day, however. Nor that of the other countries competing. In winning both the vault and the asymmetrical bars, together with the individual total, Teodora took the Japanese Cup for Romania, while Georgeta added to the triumph with a gold for the floor and a silver for the bars.

Eagerly awaiting Teodora's return, Nadia could not have been more delighted for her with three gold medals to add to a steadily growing total. Nadia's second cabinet was filling up, but Teodora's collection was not really so far behind. . . .

The next and most important event of the year in the gymnasts' calendar was the National Championships, which were to be held for three days at the end of October in Bacău.

It is only on such occasions that it is possible to appreciate the

The first ever 'Perfect 10'

extent of the concentration throughout Romania on the development of women's gymnastics. The clubs and schools are carefully nurtured and supervised in the many large centres, and the 'antremori'* can send their top teams and individual young stars of every category to compete in an arena where the standard is of a quality to attract a large audience.

The antremori – all of them professors with a sports and physical training degree† – are almost invariably appointed in pairs: a man and a woman. The man, in addition to his highly specialized technical knowledge, has the strength to catch and hold his young trainees while correcting a position. The woman, with the same basic qualifications, can bring artistry to their coaching. For this reason preference in top positions is always given to married applicants such as Bela and Marta. But with the ever-increasing demand and the considerable number of coaches that are assigned to the larger of the clubs and schools, there is no shortage of jobs and no young graduate has to wait for the chance to prove his worth in his chosen career.

Four years having elapsed since the selection of the team who went the Munich Olympics, the National Championships at Bacău were providing a similar opportunity for the selection of girls to go to Montreal.

A number of the contenders had already distinguished themselves, both in national and international contests, and the competition promised to be even stiffer than usual. All eyes, however, were on the young Comaneci who – now the European Champion and, as such, the darling of them all – must surely be a first choice. But, she still had to prove with her performance that she had lost nothing of the skill that made her one of Romania's top gymnasts.

Nadia did not disappoint them. Not only did she win the championship, but she made history in Romanian gymnastics by being awarded the first ever 'perfect 10' for her fantastic double back, Arabian front and a double full somersault in her floor discipline. From now on, this slim little thirteen-year-old girl, from her simple background, was to carry the hopes of the whole country to the coming Olympics.

Came the Christmas holidays and yet another New Year, with everyone's thoughts now on the all-important month of July. . . .

But first there was a contest for the star gymnasts from all centres at

---

* Trainers.
† The course at a university such as Bucharest is four years.

The first ever 'Perfect 10'

The first 'perfect 10'. Bacău, October 1975.

the 23 August* – a major sports complex in Bucharest – where, in winning the gold medal for the floor and every apparatus, Nadia was now conceded the title of Absolute Champion of Romania.

This was followed by yet another formidable success at the Sala Floreasca, before the team from Gheorghiu-Dej set off on a tour that was to blaze a trail through North America. Beginning in London in mid-February with a winning score for Nadia of 78.25, they flew on to Canada, where they were given a vociferous welcome in the English- and German-speaking town of Kitchener. Here the press was disappointing. There was a certain lack of credence in the judges' marking, which not only showered Nadia with the six perfect 10s that she knew she did not deserve, but were equally generous to other competitors, so that the standard of the meeting was lowered and left the Romanians non-plussed and a little uncomfortable.

From there they proceeded to Tucson, Arizona. The trip presented itself to the girls as a wonderful opportunity of seeing the world with its various cultures and peoples, and they were thrilled with the wonder of it all!

After yet another win, they travelled on to the final and more intimidating goal of the contest for the American Cup in New York. Here much was naturally expected from the little paragon. A survey had been conducted by the American press at the end of 1975, which had selected her as the World's Sportswoman of the Year. There was an enormous demand for tickets. According to the *International Gymnast Magazine*:

> Madison Square Gardens hummed with excitement as Comaneci and America's own Kathy Howard stole the show. When she left the famous edifice, Nadia took with her two perfect 10s, one acquired on the first day with her piked Tsukahara vault and the second for her fluid floor exercise in the Finale. As expected, she also took the all-round title with her excellent score of 39.70. She was not there to prove, but to display, her uncanny sense of grace, skill and technique.

Bela was a proud man indeed, as he left the famous Madison Square Gardens for the last time to escort his young team back to their hotel. The American win had been the grande finale to an eminently successful tour which had seen Nadia first in every contest and Teodora a close second. Poor Teodora! For while those in the

---

* A second example of a place being named after a commemorative date.

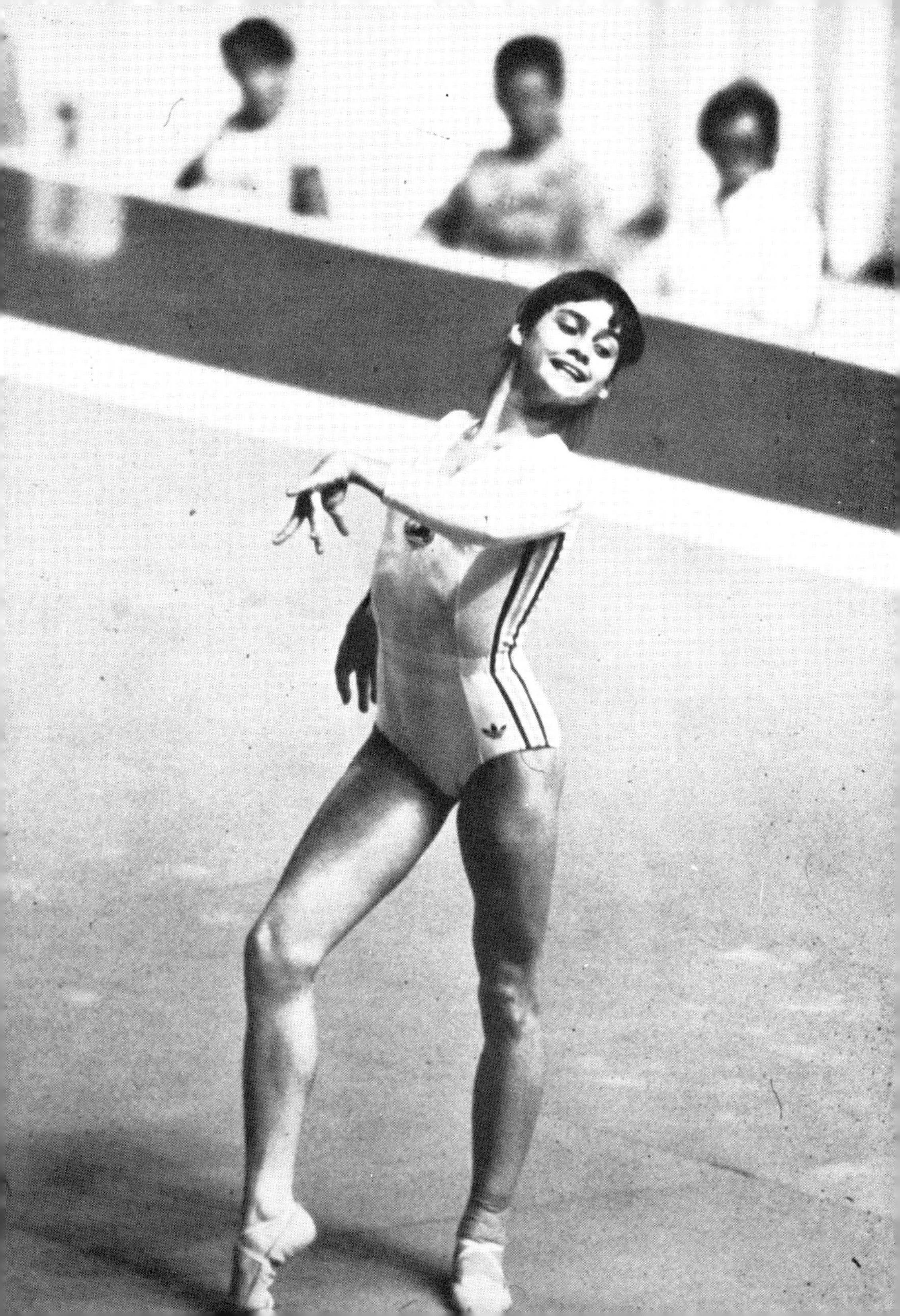

The first ever 'Perfect 10'

Gimnastica would say that there was little to choose between them as brilliant gymnasts, it was now invariably Nadia who brought that touch of genius to her performance that was needed to beat her friend and keenest adversary. Not that Teodora was showing the smallest signs of giving up the fight – which, in a strange way, seems to add a spice to their friendship.

When the tour ended nobody was sorry to be going home. Seven weeks away was long enough, and they were all of them anxious to see their families, to present the small gifts they had purchased during the journey and, most of all, to be home again.

Stefania and Emilia greeted their young daughters with open arms. They had missed them, and Gheorghe was worried that Nadia should have been so long away from school. With three months to go before the Romanian contingent would be leaving for Montreal, he was relieved when it was decided that Nadia was not to go to London to defend her title in the Champions All contest, but to settle down, instead, to a regular routine of study and training.

The *Daily Mirror*, as instigators of the competition, were disappointed. It was only the second year of the competition, which had been inspired by the enormous surge of interest in women's gymnastics that had resulted from the popular appeal of the fascinating little Olga Korbut. It was irritating that their first-ever champion should be failing them. They accepted the offer of Teodora Ungureanu as a substitute, but they were not really appeased. Gymnasts from everywhere wanted to see more of Comaneci, particularly with the approach of the Olympics. The Romanians had been lucky to find a girl of her ability; it was obvious, the *Mirror* thought, that they were keeping her back for the Games and sending the 'unknown' Ungureanu just to show willing.

Once again, however, they were to be surprised, for Teodora proved herself to be as astonishing as Nadia had been the year before when she took the Championship with flying colours. Marta, who had accompanied her, was overjoyed – not only for Teodora, but that Romania should triumph for a second time.

Back in Gheorghiu-Dej, Bela was concentrating on the training of the girls who had been selected for the Olympic team. Much to his gratification, there were to be four from the Gimnastica – and a fifth as a reserve. This was a change of plan from an original choice that had included Alina Goreac from the Dinamo Club, Bucharest, and the very young Cristina Itu. The team was now to be:

The different aspects of Teodora

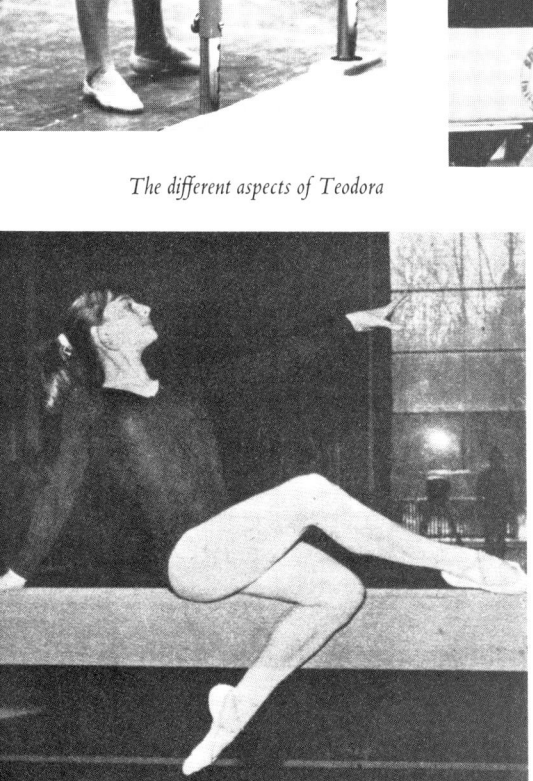

The first ever 'Perfect 10'

Nadia Comaneci	—	Gheorghiu-Dej
Teodora Ungureanu	—	,,
Mariana Constantin	—	,,
Georgeta Gabor	—	,,
*Gabriela Truşca	—	Bacău
†Anca Grigoras	—	Bucharest
Marilena Neacsu	—	Gheorghiu-Dej (reserve)

With the Olympic training ahead, it was a happy team that settled down with Nadia for an uninterrupted summer term. Their hours were to be equally divided between school and gym. Working together as a small dedicated group, they formed a strong bond of companionship. At the same time it was a pleasant break to spend long evenings lazing and playing records, or talking about the things that girls everywhere like to talk about, or cooking or sewing and generally amusing themselves about the house. Stefania could not have been happier with the new order of things, since it seemed to bring Nadia closer to her.

For in spite of the fact that mothers around could envy her for Nadia's talent and extraordinary success, there were times when she worried that she and Nadia seemed to be living in different worlds, she with her humdrum life at home and in the office, and Nadia with her gymnastics and her frequent visits to countries which, to Stefania, were just names on a map. For she learned little of them from Nadia. Still as uncommunicative as she always has been, Nadia hates to be questioned. She will come back from a trip as if she had never been away, with nothing whatsoever to say once her carefully chosen presents have been distributed. While she shows no lack of love for her mother, her life at the gym has remained the focal point of her existence.

Nevertheless she loves to come home, and to be in the room that Stefania has decorated and furnished for her to make it very much her own.

But perhaps with a lull in the series of contests, now is the time to tell a little more of Nadia's immediate surroundings and of the people around her. . . .

---

* Gabriela, at 19, is training for a physical culture degree at Bacău. Mircea and Marina Bibire coach her gymnastics.

† Anca Grigoras, who, it will be remembered, was an original member of The Flame, is reading languages and physical culture at the University of Bucharest. She is also 19.

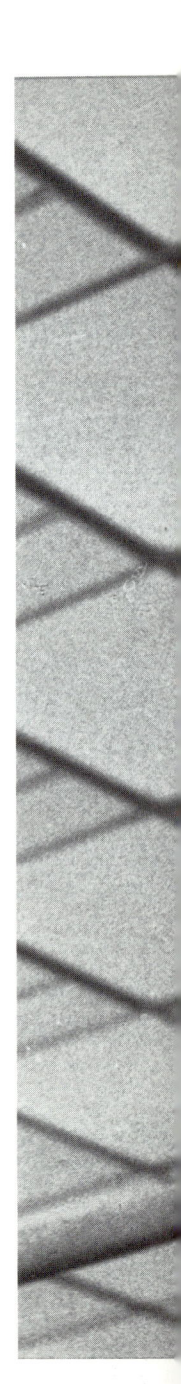

The first ever 'Perfect 10'

Nadia poses in the family flat.

8 NADIA AND TEODORA AT HOME

Stefania Comaneci is a pretty woman, small and slim, with wavy brown hair that frames her face attractively. She has brown eyes – the bronze brown of Nadia's – and a serious expression with a ready smile. She is very feminine and dresses well, knitting with a fine wool the simple, elegant cardigans and jerseys that suit her. In addition to her 'service' – the job that has her working in the office at the Sports Club for several hours each day – she is a natural homemaker.

The Comaneci flat is on the first floor of a twelve-story block of flats which, like every other, is set amid encircling greenery. Reached by a utilitarian concrete staircase, it is larger than the flat the family occupied when Nadia was a baby. This is probably because Nadia's trophies and the privacy she needs to rest require the extra space. Now there are four rooms, one of which is the sitting-room-cum-dining room. Not very large – approximately twelve feet by ten feet – it has attractive cabinets at either side, each with shelves for the great array of silver and other trophies of all shapes and sizes, and the 104 medals, 45 of which are gold. Their brightly coloured ribbons, from which they were suspended about her neck, lend an added brightness to the shining metal.

On the wall there is a quaint picture of an intensely serious-looking toddler – Nadia at two years of age. Also on the walls, and climbing high above the cabinets, are the green shining leaves of vines and other house plants that are to be found in most Romanian homes. Tall vases hold flowers at which one has to glance twice to see that they are artificial. A long sofa with bright cushions and a dining table with its chairs complete the furniture of the room which, bright and cheerful, is the centre of the family home.

A narrow hallway leads to Nadia's bedroom, where Stefania has used her favourite red for the cleverly draped satin pelmet and curtains

Stefania Comaneci

at the window. The bed also picks up the colour with a figured red-and-beige fitted cover. On the bed, just as on every well-polished piece of furniture in the room, there are dolls of all sizes and representative of many nationalities. Nadia's international family. Some of them are beautiful indeed, especially a Japanese lady; but the only one she takes to the hostel with her when she has to stay the night is the baby doll given to her in Montreal, which cries realistically when its comforter is taken from its small, rosebud mouth.

A poster painting of her on the wall was given to her in America by the artist Katsu Moriyama – who is also a writer and a gymnast. She is very fond of it. Drawers hold the stamps of which she is an avid collector, and the whole room, small as it is, is tastefully furnished and charming, reflecting Nadia herself who, like her mother, is meticulously neat and careful with her possessions.

Nadia is not yet as interested in clothes as she no doubt will be when she is a little older. She leaves that to Mariana Constantin and Marilena Neacsu, who delight to pore over the fashion magazines they pick up as they pass through various airports. For Nadia and Teodora it is always their sports clothes that count – their ski wear that must be well-cut and colourful, and their sweaters, leotards and track suits. These are all-important. A special favourite – which, once again, is a vivid scarlet – is the one that Nadia 'swopped' at an

92

Nadia and Teodora at home

The inseparable gymnasts both love trophies and souvenirs. Nadia is unrestrained in her affection for the dolls.

international contest. It has JAPAN in broad white letters across the back.

It is in their track suits that Nadia and Teodora are familiar figures in Gheorghiu-Dej, cycling out of the town on their way to the surrounding countryside, or walking together, engrossed in the discussion of the moment, as they make for the gym or the school, or traverse the short distance between their two homes.

The Ungureanu flat, not far from the Comaneci's, is in a similar block. It is smaller, but with three rooms now, including Teodora's bedroom, which contains her dolls and treasures. The sitting room, once again, is a small museum for the impressive number of her trophies and medals.

Emilia, a friendly, motherly woman, has made Teodora the centre of her existence since babyhood and has a drawer full of snapshots of her: Teodora at the creche with other adorable infants; Teodora a fairy in a tu-tu at her dancing-class display; Teodora at a tea-party; Teodora, in fact, at every stage of her young life. A collection made over the years, such as is made by many another fond parent, it has meant much to Emilia, who, a widow with her one ewe lamb, is endearingly and justifiably proud of her pretty young daughter's hard-earned success.

The Gimnastica High School is a flower-bordered, sunny

building set near the blocks of flats and within a short distance of the Sports Club and the hostel. It is light and airy with its off-white walls and polished wooden staircase and corridors. Potted plants are placed in odd corners, and the children's paintings form a small art gallery in a section to themselves. Uncluttered and spacious, the school, despite the modernity of its design and its 395 pupils, has the warm atmosphere of being lived in by an out-size family. Every child is very much an individual, with a special programming of her hours between school and gym, her progress at each being carefully noted in her official report. A special relationship is thus built up through the years between her and her young teachers, with affection and respect on both sides.

At this time, Nadia was in the eighth class of twelve, her favourite lessons being literature, French, English and chemistry. Mrs Pop says that while her continual trips have prevented her being top of her class she is invariably near it. The best marks she ever had were during this uninterrupted period, her specialized training with Bela seeming to increase her powers of concentration on her studies.

The family atmosphere, which is both surprising and unique, is present again in the gym, where the girls of all ages are undeniably happy. Their self-discipline and dedication to the work they love appears to be encouraged rather than enforced by their coaches. From the eager little seven- and eight-year-olds – the 'tinies' – and the middle set who vie with each other for places in the junior teams and could

Teodora and Nadia at the entrance to the Gimnastica High School

94

well be the Nadias and the Teodoras of the future, to the senior teams and the all-important 'national set', they all take an enormous pride in the Gheorghiu-Dej Gimnastica.

With the many trainers of these up-and-coming stars optimistic of their chances in the international arena at an early age, it could be interesting to watch some of those of whom they are most hopeful. The blonde and charming Florica Dobre and her husband Florin, for instance, are pinning their hopes on Dana Craciun, Corina Sasu and Dumitrita Turner; while Maria Florescu and Mihai Agoston have the tinies Florina Agachi, Neli Marcu and Liliana Vilcu; and Elena Duicu and others are looking to Mihaela Infrim, Lenuta Ghioane and Romena Rosoga. Impossible, however, to list them all, and one can only cross one's fingers for them and wish them well. Mrs Mili, a fascinating and infinitely lovable person, with her olive face and the expressive brown eyes – which can sparkle with laughter, gleam with interest or soften in sympathy – adores them all.

*   *   *   *   *   *

The spring had passed, and with the warm summer days of June tension was mounting in Romania with the final preparations for the Montreal Olympics. The team and individual contestants who went to Munich having returned with a total of 16 medals – one more than from Mexico in '68 – it seemed not unreasonable to be hoping for more from Montreal; particularly as Mrs Mili's new concept had gathered momentum so as to make women's gymnastics, in Professor Chisoiu's opinion, the apex of Romanian sport.

But in an atmosphere of quiet tranquility in Gheorghiu-Dej there had been little to distract the team from the daily routine that had been planned to keep them on an even keel. Day followed day, with each of the five working in turn with Bela and Marta before going on to Geza Poszar and Carol Stabişevschi; and with Mrs Mili and Atanasia – better known as Sica – popping in at odd times to see how it was going. Beneath the surface there was a seething excitement throughout the whole of the Gimnastica as, coaches and gymnasts alike, they watched the Olympic team at their training – and a great sense of pride as Nadia worked steadily through her 'difficulties' with an ease and fluency that was approaching perfection.

'Go home!' Bela would order the tinies as they peeped, open-mouthed, around the door that leads to the changing rooms. But the gruffness of his tone would be belied by the smile with which he listened to their swift departure. At seven and eight years old they

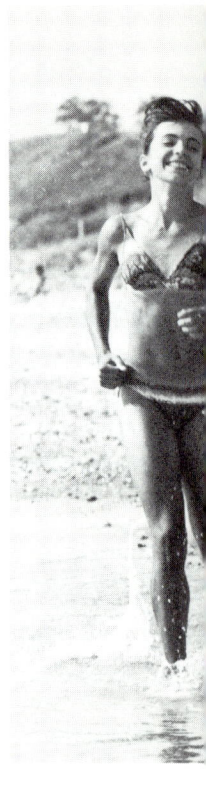

Bela and baby Andrea at Mangalia with Marilena Neacsu, Mariana Constantin and (right) Nadia.

were very small – just thrilled little children who couldn't have enough of Nadia, their idol.

'You're doing well, Nadia,' he told her one day, a little too casually. 'Keep it up and you'll do even better.'

Nadia stared for a moment before giving him one of her rare smiles.

'You said that to me before,' she told him. 'A long time ago.'

'Did I?' Bela asked her happily. 'Ah, well . . . Come along, young Ungureanu, it's your turn.'

Teodora was also doing splendidly. Pondering on their chances as he hurried home to play with his baby Andrea before she went to bed, Bela considered that there was very little to choose between his two stars. Teodora, still a keen rival, could be as good as Nadia on the bars and the beam, and Geza Poszar was delighted with her grace on the floor. There was little doubt that each of them was going to put up a formidable opposition in the Forum in Montreal – where they would be performing before an audience of 17,000. But what were the Russians likely to do? Kim had been brilliant at the pre-Olympics and Tourischeva would surely be at her best with her final appearance before her retirement. What, too, of Olga Korbut, whom they had yet to meet. And what of East Germany and Hungary, with Angelika Hellmann, Gitta Escher and Marta Egervari? But confident that this time Romania had a team that would take some beating, Bela was content to wait and see.

The girls had been measured for the suits they were to wear as their country's uniform, and they were all intrigued with the colour. The lilac blue was perfect for the cerise which predominated in the pretty, multi-coloured silk shirts; and the shoulder bags and shoes of a light tan added to the simple and attractive general effect. The uniforms soon arrived, together with the white leotards with their red, yellow

97

Nadia and Teodora at home

and blue stripes at either side continuing along the under arm, and with the blazers and sweaters and other kit called for a trying-on session that seemed to bring reality to a dream. They were going to the Olympics! They had known it for months, and yet it was only now, with the colours and the badges that were to show them as Romanians and, as such, the chosen representatives of their country, that the responsibility of all that could be expected of them brought with it a sudden sense of apprehension. To other contests they had travelled happily enough, but this was different – another thing altogether. But it was only a momentary panic and passed as quickly as it had come, in the pride that was to replace it, and amid the excited chatter that accompanied the gathering up of the individual items.

It was not so with Stefania, who had been there to watch. Realizing too that the Olympics was a world event, she was fearful for Nadia. With her continued success, particularly in the European Championship, surely everyone would be expecting her to win in Montreal? But supposing, this time, something should go wrong? Supposing she should lose her grip on the bars or her balance on the beam? What would it do to her enigmatic young daughter to fail to achieve her ultimate goal in a career to which she had devoted the whole of her life? Obsessed with the anxiety – which might have made Gheorghe chide her as a 'born worrier' – from this time on Stefania found herself looking for even the smallest sign of nerves in Nadia.

On the night before they were due to leave, with her packing finished and the dolls ousted from her bed Nadia appeared to be asleep when Stefania went in to her. Hoping for a last, quiet chat, Stefania had wanted to reassure her that it did not matter a jot if, this time, she should be beaten by Nelli Kim or Olga Korbut, or anyone else. She would have done her best and that was all that could be expected of anybody. Afraid even to drop a kiss on her young daughter's forehead in case it could wake her, Stefania sighed as she closed the door noiselessly behind her. She was not to know until the following morning that, too excited to sleep until the early hours, Nadia had lain awake rehearsing her disciplines. It was not that she was nervous, only that she liked to go over the timing of every movement, from a half beat for a flick of the fingers to the semibreve and pause that goes for a handstand on the top of the asymmetrical bars. Lost in the concentration that comes naturally to her, she had been all unaware of her mother's coming in. 'But that is Nadia', Stefania will say with a shrug of her shoulders and a whimsical smile.

The Olympic party – Marta, Georgeta, Luminita (reserve), Teodora, Nadia, Bela, Marilena (reserve), Mrs Mili, Mariana, Gabriela Truşca and Anca Grigoras.

9 MONTREAL 1976

The girls looked strangely grown-up in their trim new suits the morning they left Gheorghiu-Dej for Montreal – a patch of blue in the centre of the crowd that had gathered to see them off and wish them luck as they waited for their transport to arrive with Bela and Marta and Stabişevschi.

So many people were there – families and friends and neighbours with their children, the little girls with their white hair ribbons, and the small boys who, with their naval-type peaked school caps, were very like those who had taught Nadia her first handstands. Now she was everybody's Nadia – the girl who had brought the European

99

Montreal 1976

Championship to Romania and who, with Teodora, was one of the brightest hopes for the Olympics.

Emilia was endeavouring to find a way through the congestion to give her daughter a final hug, while Stefania, no longer so worried now that the sun was shining and in the general excitement and merriment, was listening to Gheorghe and Bela. With Montreal eight hours behind Bucharest, they were working out the times when those at home would be able to see the gymnasts on television. It seemed that they would be up half the night, but nobody minded – they weren't going to miss it for the world. . . .

But then it was time to leave for the assembly point, where they were to meet Anca Grigoras and Gabriela Truşca, with Mrs Mili and Sica; and where, as the women's gymnastic team, they would be just a small unit among the cream of Romania's athletes. Then on to the airport, where there was nothing of stern officialdom today. Busier than ever with its milling youth, it seemed almost to be *en fête*. A great day, indeed! And one that could not happen again for another four years.

The girls were used to travelling on a scheduled air flight to their various destinations, and the chartered plane was, in itself, a novelty, without the usual anonymity of fellow-passengers. The athletes were all of their own kind. Difficult to tell apart in their identical uniforms, they were all eager to proclaim themselves Romanians.

But such a fever pitch of gaiety and excitement could not be kept up and soon an air of sleepy contentment prevailed throughout the aircraft. Glancing round at her little brood, Mrs Mili studied them one by one – Mariana chatting softly to her friend, Marilena; the clever little Georgeta who was soon to give up her gymnastics as a main study and switch to an academic career; Anca Grigoras, always a favourite; Gabriela Truşca from Bacău; and Teodora, who invariably slept almost from take-off to landing.

Nadia, whose eyes never miss the smallest detail and who loves to ask questions, was looking anxiously towards the air hostess, and tapped Mrs Mili's shoulder as she approached. Mrs Mili shook her head.

'No, I don't really think we should today, Nadia,' she said. 'Not with so many of us. . . .'

Nadia was disappointed. Fascinated with flying, she often coaxes Mrs Mili to ask if she may visit the flight-deck. The first occasion was on a Boeing two years ago when she intrigued the British Airways captain by questioning him about the instruments.

'You wouldn't have expected it of a little girl like that,' he was to comment later. 'Passengers are not generally allowed on the flight-deck, but on the odd occasion that VIPs come along they usually content themselves with looking ahead as we pass through the clouds. But this tiny thing was far more interested in my job, and, in spite of the language difficulty, we managed somehow to communicate. Most of all, she was enchanted with the inertial navigation system that hands out information like a computer, giving the air and wind speed or danger signals, or maybe the exact time to a half a second that we are due to land – almost anything you like to ask it. She loved it.'

Nadia was not to know that it was to be her turn to fascinate the captain when, happening to be in Montreal on the first day of the Olympics, he was to see her first appearance in the Forum.

'I can't tell you how proud I was,' he said later. 'My little girl! – I could scarcely believe it!'

Landing in Montreal, it was no time at all before they were all installed in the athletes' village, where they were happy to meet many old friends. Among them were the Russians: Tourischeva, of whom Nadia is a great admirer, and Nelli Kim. Then there were the East Germans and the Hungarians and the beautiful little girls from Japan, including Satoko Okazaki and Sakiko Mozawa.

Bela was enquiring about their training the week before the Opening Day and was delighted to find that, as there were three splendidly equipped gymnasiums, every team was to be allowed as much as three hours a day. Apart from this, there was the swimming and the tennis and many other things to do and to see.

But even though the colourful community life of the village was a delightful experience, it was still the hours spent at their training that, for the girls, were the focal point of each day. This was the time they would be together in their own environment with Bela. He was no longer necessary as the blonde giant who was to catch them in his arms. With an equal strength in his imperturbability, he was the familiar father-figure who would direct their concentration where it was needed and instil a feeling of confidence that all was well.

For the final two days before the competition, the teams were allowed to train on the podium itself in the great Forum. Here, the phenomenal increase in the popularity of women's gymnastics – which make it a rival to ballet – was shown by the fact that every seat was taken for the actual games, while the street outside was packed with people who were anxious to pay to see the girls training. Many were turned away, and the arena was filled on each occasion.

Montreal 1976

Sitting among the audience to watch the girls from East Germany, Nadia and Teodora were impressed with the quiet concentration of everyone around. It was an Olympic audience – and one that they would see duplicated on Monday with the first of the women's contests. Teodora was relieved and happy to find nothing intimidating in the vastness of the crowd, but only a warmth and encouragement.

Then came the day of days – the Opening Day of the 1976 Montreal Olympics! It was an unforgettable occasion, both for the veterans, moved by its simplicity and beauty, and for the young who were there for the first time and were lost in the wonder of it all. Without seeming to isolate themselves in their proud patriotism the athletes paraded in the stadium behind their countries' flags. There was an atmosphere of world unity, regardless of creed or colour, or of differing languages and customs – almost as if Pandora's box had never been opened....

Tired, but happy beyond words to have been a part of it, the young Romanians went early to bed to be ready for the morrow.

* * * * * *

The long-awaited contest to determine the world's greatest women gymnasts had started. There were six gold medals to be won: one for the team award; one each for the girls with top marks in the individual competitions on each piece of apparatus – bars, beam, vault – and on the floor; and, most glamorous of all, the gold for the Overall Champion.

There were 86 competitors – six in each of the twelve teams allowed by the Olympic rule – together with the fourteen top gymnasts whose attainments in the international arena qualified them to enter as individuals. Among these were three British girls – Avril Lennox, the British Champion, Barbara Slater and Susan Cheeseborough – though the British team as a whole failed to qualify. The teams represented were Bulgaria, Italy, West Germany, East Germany, Hungary, USA, Japan, USSR, Canada, Czechoslovakia, Netherlands and Romania.

The Russian team – consisting of Tourischeva, the world champion, Kim, Korbut, Saadi, Grazova and the minute Maria Filatova – were all world-class and it was generally accepted that they would prove unbeatable. They began well, with a good score for the first of their compulsory exercises, on the asymmetrical bars, and they were waiting for the Romanians to finish theirs on the beam. Teodora

The opening ceremony at the Montreal Olympics, 1976

had been awarded a 9.75, but it was Nadia Comaneci – the European Champion – who held their anxious attention as she crossed the podium to acknowledge the judges.

Writing in *The Gymnast*, John Goodbody says that many women gymnasts dislike to start a competition on the beam – 'because it has such a premium on meticulous skill.' He goes on to say:

> But Nadia did not hesitate. She went through her routine without apparent error. On her handstand she lifted her legs overhead so gradually that it appeared as if she could not have the momentum to reach the position. But she did – and then she marked it there so slowly as if she wanted to stress the

Montreal 1976

smoothness of the action before proceeding with the exercise. The applause she received was tumultuous. It was louder than anything the Russians had got on the asymmetrical bars. The Russian squad turned away, ostensibly to collect their bags. But the applause had plainly embarrassed them. They knew then that Nadia was as proficient as she had been in winning the European Championships last year and that, on this form, none of them was likely to beat her. This was confirmed by the mark she achieved – 9.90 – and perhaps even more importantly by the fact that she was being clapped by the other gymnasts in the competitors' enclosure. Nadia chose this moment to salute everyone's appreciation. She was as confident as she was immaculate.

Rivals. Nadia, left, and Olga, right.

The Russians followed on the beam. Olga, still with her gay, gamin smile, was the best of them, showing some of the skill she had displayed at Munich. She scored 9.80 – .10 less than Nadia and .5 more than Teodora – while Tourischeva and Kim each got 9.40.

The Romanians went to the asymmetrical bars. Teodora gave a splendid performance – she excels at the bars. She was marked 9.90 – a mark that was to be consistent throughout the entire competition. Then came Nadia. Springing effortlessly to the lower bar, in a moment her slim sinuous body was weaving a pattern in between and around the bars with a silken softness, until, seeming to throw herself into space, she performed her magnificent and dangerous Radochla somersault – 'from the high bar to the high'.* And now, with a 'clear hip circle backwards' she was poised, pencil slim and straight, in the handstand which she holds for longer than would seem humanly possible. It is an unbelievable feat of balance and control, which never fails to leave the audience open-mouthed with astonishment. Finally came the famous Comaneci dismount – stoop on the high bar, underswing with half turn, and a back somersault to the mat below.

*Quoted from Pauline Prestidge, ex-National Team Coach in her book *Gymnastic Coaching*. Pauline Prestidge also says that Nadia 'was the very first girl to show that the Radochla can be performed from the high bar to the high. A fantastic achievement. . . . Henceforth this new version of the Radochla will be known as "The Comaneci".'

105

Pausing only to acknowledge with a brief nod the vociferous applause, Nadia proceeded to leave the podium with the grace and dignity of a young Queen. This only added to the feeling that here was something different from anything that had ever been seen before. Rejoining her team, she remained standing. Then, turning to regard the scoreboard, she unconsciously betrayed a little of herself in raising a finger to rub her nose at the corner of her left eye – an endearing little habit she has when engrossed. When the board showed a perfect 10 – *the first ever in the history of Olympic gymnastics* – there came first a gasp and then renewed applause, which was all but deafening, from 17,000 pairs of hands – a roar that was heard by millions upon millions of television viewers throughout the world. In just a few moments an unknown fourteen-year-old schoolgirl had rocketed herself to fame. . . .

But even while the individual placings for the compulsory exercises showed Nadia – with 39.35 points – ahead of Tourischeva and Teodora, who were equal with 38.85, the Russians were still leading for the team medal; their combined total being 194.20 against the Romanians 192.70. The East Germans, with their stars Escher and Kische, were lying third with 191.60. It was the marks for the 'voluntaries' to follow which, added to those already awarded, would determine the winning team. But Kim and Korbut had been only fractionally behind Tourischeva and Teodora, and it was going to need a *tour de force* for the Romanian team to overtake them.

Montreal 1976

The famous Comaneci dismount, drawn by Atanasia.

They couldn't do it. But maybe, in the light of things to come, the fates were smiling on Tourischeva in granting her a final triumph before her retirement.

Even so, Nadia, too, had triumphed! She had won another two perfect 10's for the beam and the bars and a total for her voluntaries of 39.70 points – only three-tenths of a point short of a maximum! Frank Taylor states that no other gymnast in history has ever scored so high. 'I have had the privilege of reporting many great moments in sport all over the world,' he says, 'but never quite like this!'

But could she keep it up, was the question every sports writer was asking. This was Monday, and there were four days to go before the brilliant Tourischeva might be fighting to retain her world championship at the finals for the Overall Championship. Had Nadia's extraordinary performance been a once-in-a-lifetime affair? Or could she do it again, to challenge the supremacy of the twenty-four-year-old Russian on the eve of her retirement?

Nadia and Teodora worked hard with Bela on Tuesday – the day before the battle for the individual medals and the championship. Meanwhile Nadia was being besieged by the media. She couldn't move for reporters and cameras. Bela kept her out of sight as far as possible, but there were still the other Olympic contestants whom she met in the dining hall, and who clamoured to speak to the young heroine. Precious McKenzie, the tiny South African weightlifter, was among them. 'She smiled,' he said, 'but she's a very shy little girl!'

The Russian challenge – Ludmila Tourischeva, above, and Nelli Kim, below.

Then once again they were in the arena. Of the original entry of 86 girls, there were now only 36 who would compete in the preliminaries for the Thursday finals. At the end of the day the number would be considerably smaller, with only the top six girls on each separate apparatus eligible to compete on the morrow for the individual medals and the overall award. Once again the 'preliminaries' would start with the compulsories and go on to the voluntaries. The scores for each would be added and then divided to give a carry-forward figure under a preliminary heading (see p. 132). The final result showed Nadia still in the lead with 39.525 points, but with Ludmila Tourischeva and Nelli Kim dangerously near tying second, only four-tenths of a point behind.

The final day of the women's gymnastics, Thursday 22 July 1976, saw crowds of people milling around the entrance to the Forum, begging to be allowed in, if only to stand. Frank Taylor writes: '... spivs, who fought a running battle of wits against police and security services, were asking and getting $100 for a $16 ticket.' It seemed as if the whole of Montreal had been caught up in the drama that was to be enacted in the arena between the beautiful and popular Ludmila Tourischeva, who had reigned supreme for many years, and the tiny slip of a girl, from a relatively unimportant country, who was seeking to depose her.

108

Montreal 1976

Montreal 1976

Now only eleven girls were left to compete. The Russians – Tourischeva, Kim, and Korbut: the Romanians – Comaneci and Ungureanu: the East Germans – Hellmann, Kische, Escher and Dombeck: Egervari from Hungary and Pohludkova from Czechoslovakia. Only Nadia had qualified to enter for all of the four individual medals. She had won both the bars and the beam at the preliminaries – with yet another two perfect 10s. She had also come third on the floor and fourth in the vault. Kim and Tourischeva could each of them enter for three. Kim, at this stage, appeared to be doing better than Tourischeva. She had achieved a perfect 10 for a truly magnificent vault and had beaten her compatriot into second place on the floor. But Tourischeva – with her beloved coach, Vladislav Rastorotsky, to boost her confidence – was in no way dismayed. The final was the final, and she meant to fight – and to fight hard!

She gave a superbly elegant performance on the asymmetrical bars – with Rastorotsky standing as near as possible to her (male coaches are not allowed on the podium). There was loud applause, followed by silence – as everyone waited for the score. Then came the booes from a discontented audience, who had expected more than a lukewarm 9.85 and seemed to want the Russian girl to win the championship as the crowning glory of a fine career. . . .

Nadia was to follow her on the bars. The booes continued until she acknowledged the judges. This might have been off-putting. But not to one with Nadia's stamina. Seemingly unperturbed, as she rubbed her hands with magnesia, she once again gave a splendid sequence of her most intricate feats, including the new Radochla. It won her her sixth perfect 10! Tourischeva shrugged her shoulders as she turned to her coach. He only smiled and gave her a 'thumbs up', as if to say: 'You aren't beaten yet!'

And then Nadia went to the beam. Thrilling as her performance had been before (it was her favourite apparatus), this final time it was sheer magic. It was not only her incredible agility and balance, her grace or her meticulous precision that held the audience spellbound. For many there was so much more – something remote and intangible in the intense seriousness of her expression and her apparent unawareness of her surroundings. She was lost in concentration and a deep absorption in her rhythm and movement. There was something about her suggestive of the loneliness of a prima ballerina. Springing lightly back on to the floor, with her feet perfectly together, she paused before raising herself on a *demi-pointe* to complete her exercise. This

An apprehensive Nelli Kim watches the brilliance of Comaneci.

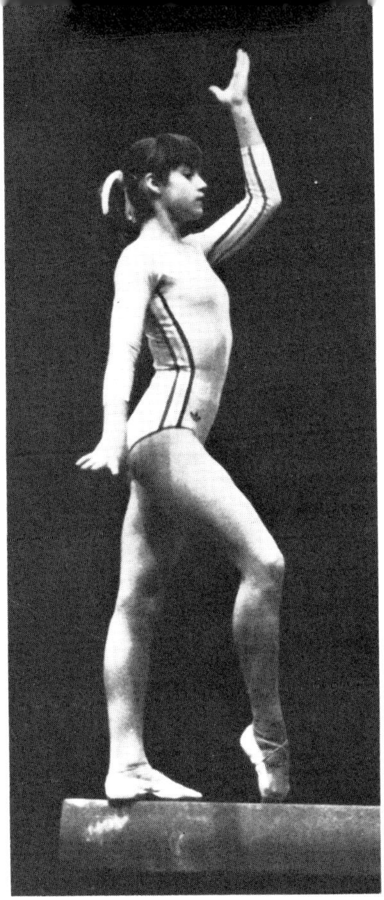
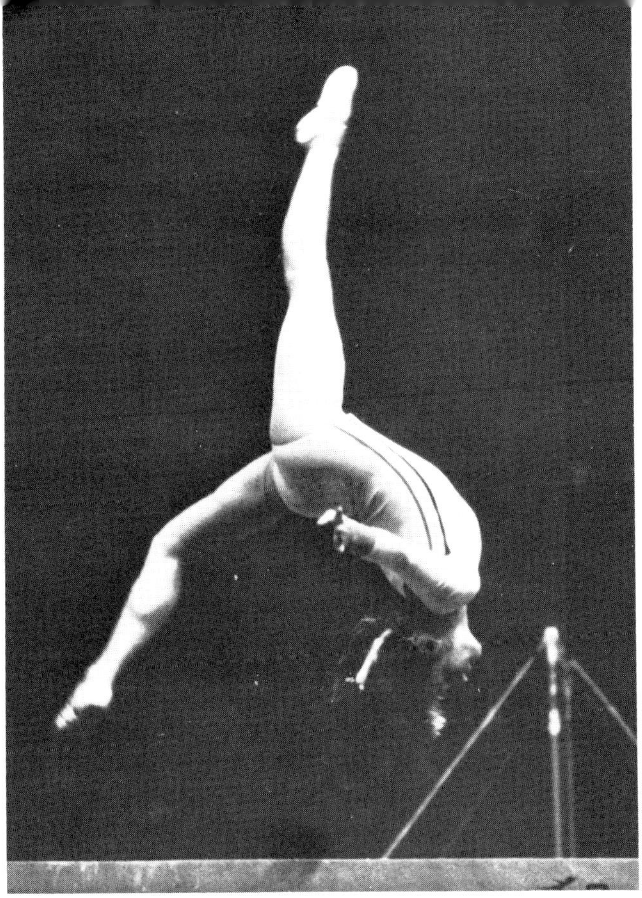
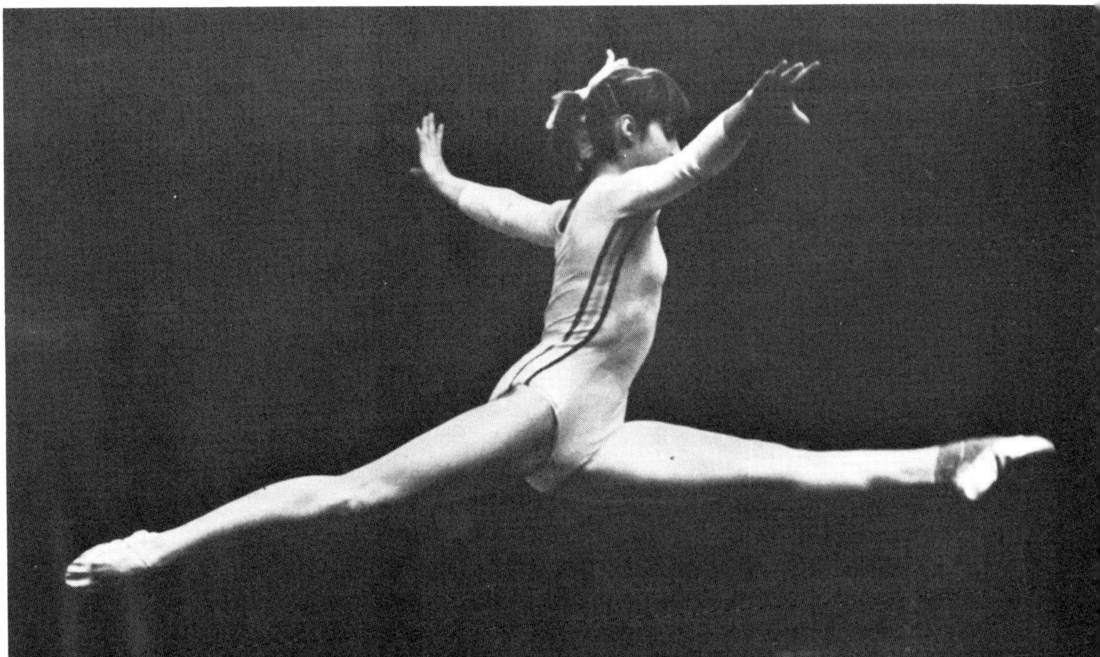

time she acknowledged the storm of clapping that followed, with a shy, quick smile. The scoreboard showed her seventh perfect 10 – it couldn't have been otherwise. . . .

Nadia had taken the golds for the beam and the bars, and Nelli Kim the gold for the vault. Now there was only the floor.

The atmosphere was tense with excitement, as sports writers and audience alike assessed the position of the leading girls. Nadia·was still ahead for the Overall Champion's medal, with a total of 69.375. But the others were close behind, with Ludmila Tourischeva 68.725, Nelli Kim 68.675 and Teodora 68.575. There was little in it, particularly between the first two girls, upon whom attention centred. The floor exercises have always been an 'ace' for Tourischeva, who over the years has become famous for the superb grace, charm and beauty that she has added to an experienced technique.

Much as everyone was fascinated by Nadia's extraordinary skill and elusive personality, there was no doubt now that most of the audience were crossing their fingers for Ludmila. It was, after all, to be her swan song. . . .

Certainly there was no sign of despair – no hint even of anxiety – as she made her way to the podium. The music had been well chosen, and she brought it to life with a fine interpretation. There was variety in her repertoire of disciplines, which resembled ballet. Even so there was something missing. A *je-ne-sais-quoi*. . . . Was it, perhaps, the youthful verve that had been so notable at Munich? Who knows? The audience gave her a long and generous applause. The scoreboard showed a 9.90, which – this time – they did not dispute.

All eyes were now upon Nadia – especially the eyes of Ludmila and the faithful Rastorotsky. Who could blame them if they hoped a little that this time her luck would desert her? Nadia had not acquired the perfection on the floor that she had on the beam and the bars. It would require no more than a tiny drop for her to be standing beside Ludmila for the silver when the flag would go up for the Overall Champion. . . .

Flinging herself into the gay Charleston that Stabişevschi had established for her, Nadia finished with a flourish and a score of 9.90 to equal that of Ludmila. No one now could beat her. Nadia Elena Comaneci, who had set her feet on the ladder of fame at such a very early age, had reached the very top! She had won the gold medal of the Overall Champion of the Olympics. . . .

But still not the individual gold for the floor – the medal which, through the years, had seemed almost to belong to Tourischeva. This

Montreal 1976

Joy and despair as Nadia Comaneci deposes the former World Champion.

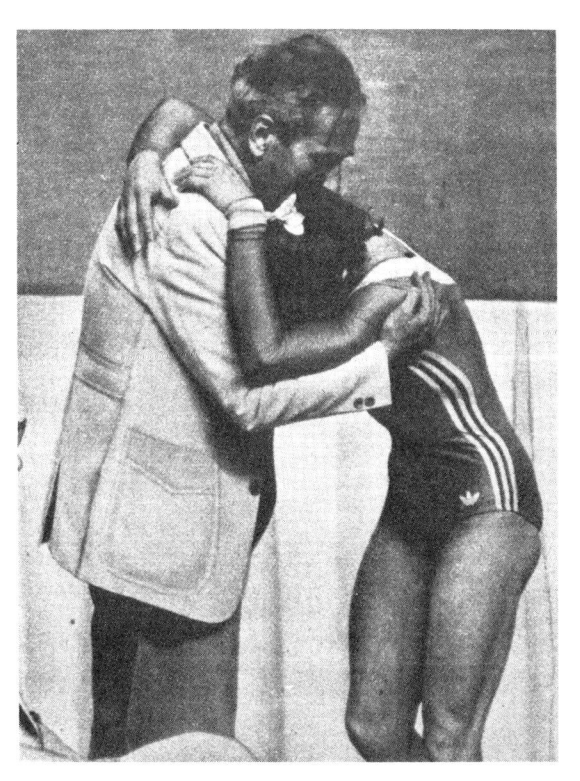

was to be stolen by Nelli Kim, who, in her eye-catching purple leotard, almost brought the house down with a breathtaking performance that won her her second perfect 10.

This wasn't all. It needed little calculation to show that Kim, with her newest score, had overtaken Ludmila, to put herself in second place in the Overall. She had won the silver medal, and the older girl was relegated to the bronze.

It was too much for poor Ludmila! Unable any longer to blink back the tears, she flung herself into her coach's arms and wept.

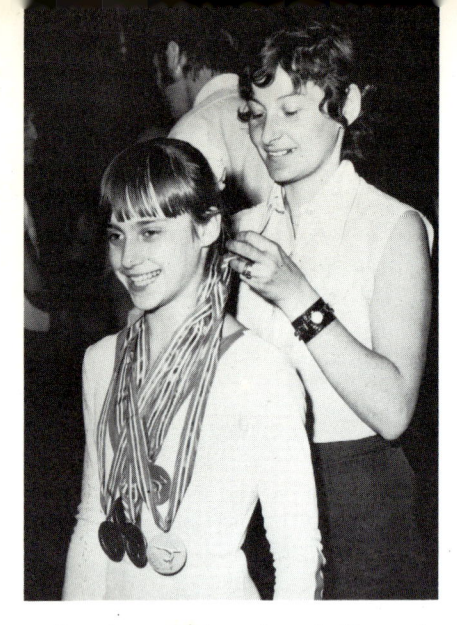

Nadia with Marta

But the tears ceased, and the ex-champion – whom no one will forget – put on a brave face as she mounted the rostrum to collect her medal. She paused to kiss the new champion – and to kiss Nelli Kim too, who was replacing her as Russia's leading woman gymnast. Then she gave her usual sweet smile and held her head high as she joined them on the platform of honour.

And what were the feelings of the little fourteen-year-old schoolgirl as she stood waiting for the flag of Romania to be hoisted to the strains of her national anthem? Those who saw her on television may remember that she wrinkled her nose a little, as if it tickled. It was not until she arrived home that she was able to say quaintly, 'I felt that I was dreaming with my eyes open. I was so happy, it was unbelievable! Only I wanted to cry for Tourischeva when she kissed me. She is a very great gymnast and a great sportswoman. I loved her for it.'

But now, with the greatest success of her career, there came the greatest pressure of all in an undreamed-of publicity – anathema to the shy, unsophisticated girl who, in aiming to be a top gymnast had never seen herself as a celebrity. Nadia tried valiantly, in the interests of her country, to disguise the fact that she was out of her depth. As she gave her stiff little answers, through an interpreter, to a barrage of questions that were invariably the same, her very youth and inexperience made her hide behind the mask of an apparent self-possession. She revealed little or nothing of her real self – a girl with an above-average intelligence, with a dry, intriguing sense of humour and a warmth and friendliness for those who can discuss her interests. It was sad that lack of understanding should have led one journalist to

Montreal 1976

label her 'Little Miss Stonyface'. Perhaps in four years' time, at the next Olympics, when she will still be only a few months older than the effervescent and charming Olga Korbut was at Munich, Nadia will have acquired a stage presence to please him. Meanwhile, there are many who just love her as she is.

Appreciating the strain she was under with the continuous demands upon her for photographs and interviews, the Sports Council decided that, rather than wait to return with the rest of the contingent, the gymnastic team should be whisked home in a Scandinavian plane leaving the following Tuesday, 27 July. It was a wise decision, for upon arriving at Bucharest, the little champion – thrilled with her success and all that it was giving to her country, but bewildered with her new importance as 'the woman of the moment' – just flung herself into her mother's arms and burst into tears.

The returning champion has to face the Press.

Montreal 1976

But if Nadia's homecoming from Norway had won a great ovation, this time it was as if the entire population of the capital were there to greet the team on their victorious return – with their pride and joy in Nadia shining from their eyes as they cheered her as if they could never stop. Teodora, too, who with her silver and bronze medals had come fourth in the battle for the championship, with a final marking that had placed her only nine-tenths of a point lower than the champion herself! From the parkland drive from the airport to the wide boulevards of Bucharest, no Queen of Christendom with her handmaidens could have had a finer reception! As they returned by car to Gheorghiu-Dej, country folk who had walked the miles from their villages lined the highway and threw flowers for Nadia, the most popular little girl in Romania!

A victory parade delights the crowd.

Nadia larger than life

In their home town 33,000 people crowded into the sports arena. Then came the speeches and the presentations, and in the days that followed Nadia was to wish that there was an underground passage leading from her home to the gym. For now, even the dear familiarity of Gheorghiu-Dej was suddenly different, with people urging her to go to the head of the queue when shopping, and others stopping her for autographs. Nevertheless, taking the precaution of riding everywhere on her bicycle instead of walking even the smallest distance, it was not so long before, with the Olympics behind them and already looking towards other goals, life both for Nadia and the rival she still has in the indomitable Teodora, was soon to resume its normal pattern. Revelling once again in their personal contest in the gym and, with the summer holidays their freedom to pursue their other sports and the ordinary things of ordinary girls, now would seem to be the time to leave them happily content in the place they love.

But that would be to deny them the final honour that is their due when they were both to be among the most distinguished of all the contestants who had returned victorious from Montreal. For it was at a great gathering on 18 August 1976 at the splendid new Palace of Sports and Culture in Bucharest, when, in the presence of the Leaders of State and Party and amid an audience of several thousand

118

In the Palace of Sport and Culture Nadia is decorated by President Ceauşescu and with fellow gymnasts dances in traditional dress.

athletes from all over the country, they and their coaches – including Bela and Marta and Mrs Mili – were invested with the medals and awards that they had so richly deserved.

But in an atmosphere that was redolent of pride, at no time was the flourish of trumpets more impressive or the cheers louder or more prolonged than when, in a moment that marked her greatest triumph, the President, Nicolae Ceauşescu, bestowed the Gold Medal of a Hero of Socialist Labour on an overmodest little patriot, NADIA OF ROMANIA....

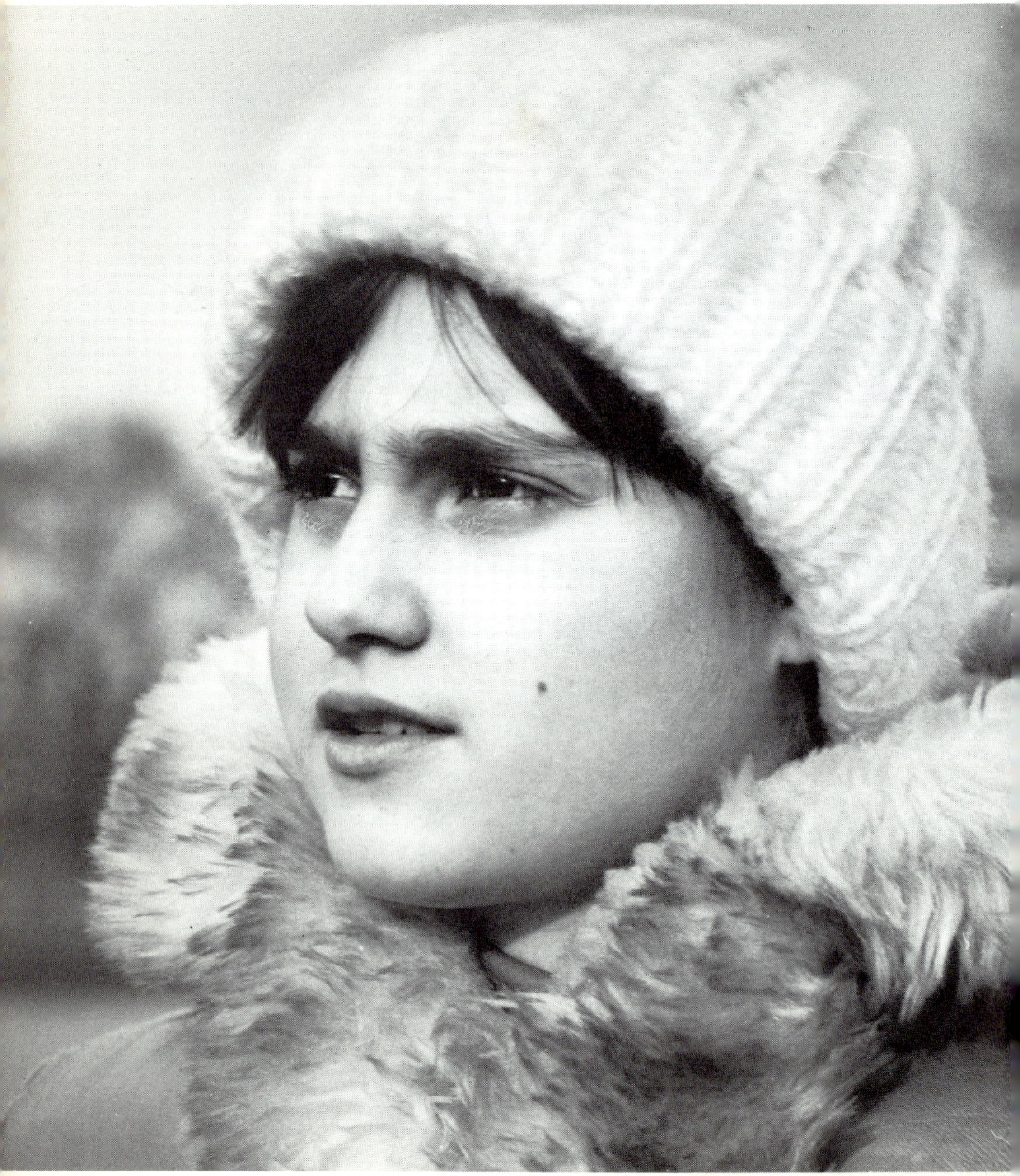

10 INTO THE FUTURE

For all those who would envy the fame of Nadia Comaneci, who at the tender age of fourteen would seem to have achieved her heart's desire, there must be the other side of the picture. To reach such a pinnacle as a gymnast after years of unremitting work is one thing, but to remain there demands an even greater dedication and stoicism. For it is not only her present rivals – the Nelli Kims of the erstwhile unbeatable USSR – or even her great friend, Teodora Ungureanu – who are out to topple the young Queen of the Castle from her throne. An equal danger lurks in the up-and-coming young gymnasts from all over the world to whom her prowess is both an inspiration and a challenge.

So it was that, following her triumphant return to Romania, when she was greeted with all the pomp and ceremony and adulation that a grateful country could bestow on their much-loved little star, Nadia soon had to come down to earth and resume the daily pattern of an arduous routine.

First, however, was the annual August holiday on the Black Sea – not quite as carefree perhaps this year, since, with her greatly increased popularity, the smiles and the greetings everywhere gave her none of the anonymity she loves. And it only needed a whisper of 'Look, there goes Nadia!' for the children to crowd around begging for autographs. But she was happy enough to lie on the sand and chat with them until, bored and wanting to relax, she would shoo them away. It was the foreign journalists who continued to pursue her with their cameras who could have her smiles vanishing and her face tightening to its strange immobility – rather as if she had closed a door upon herself and turned the key!

Then, once again, it was back to Gheorghiu-Dej and the hard grind for which she had kept herself in trim with the daily exercises

Nadia looks out on London in December 1976.

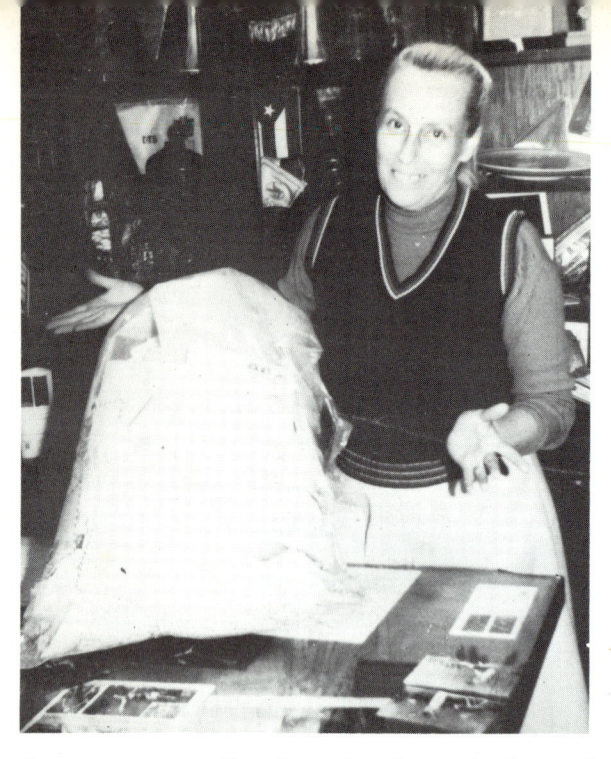

Aftermath of Montreal. Mrs Mili with some of Nadia's mail, Nadia with autograph hunters.

that come as naturally to her as breathing. And soon she was off again on her travels.

In October 1976 newspapers showed her being kissed by Princess Grace of Monaco after a gymnastics display on the French Riviera. It was here that a 'whip' in the asymmetric bars caused her to fall, and the hurt to her dignity at such a happening in front of TV cameras was greater than that of the ensuing bruises – all the more since the media were running an exaggerated story of a weight increase which, it was being said, could jeopardise her future chances. In fact the only weight she had put on was that which was in accordance with an adolescent filling out of the slim childish contours of her body and with a sudden increase in her height.

Early in November the Romanian team of Nadia, Teodora and Georgeta Gabor set off for Japan, accompanied by Bela and Mrs Mili, to compete for the Chunichi Cup in Nagoya. It was a trip that was to be adventurous from the very start. Flying first to Heathrow, where they were to be in transit, their Boeing had scarcely landed when they were told that a one-day porters' strike made it necessary for them to carry their own luggage to the British Airways Jumbo Jet. Young and strong and not overburdened, the girls thought it a great joke – though it was not one that was shared by their fellow passengers.

Then came the flight itself which, for Nadia, was entrancing. For

122

this time there was actually an invitation for interested junior passengers to go to the flight deck. There they were not only to meet the Captain of the aircraft but to have him sign the personal log books they were each given to record future flights. Nadia as a VIP received a special welcome, and much to her delight was permitted a longer than usual visit as she watched the inertial navigation system in operation as they flew over the North Pole. She was thrilled as questions and answers were exchanged in rapid succession with Anchorage in Alaska.

It was on leaving the 'plane in Tokyo that things suddenly became frightening when a seething mass of people came surging across the airfield to greet the young Olympic star. It was in vain that the police tried to keep them back. They had read of her arrival in the newspapers and were determined to catch a glimpse of her. Mrs Mili remembers the resulting chaos as something of a nightmare when they were surrounded on all sides by what appeared as a yelling mob. The police did what they could, but it was inevitable that the team should become separated. She recalls her relief when they were eventually united and safely lodged in their hotel!

From then on the trip was spoiled, since it was decided that their every movement must be closely guarded. This time there was to be no sightseeing – and that which for the girls was even worse – no shopping! Nevertheless there were compensations when the

Into the future

Romanian team swept the field at the contest. Nadia took the Chunichi Cup and the gold medal, with Teodora a close second with the silver and Georgeta third with the bronze. It was sad, indeed, for the team from the USSR, that Nelli Kim should be incapacitated with an injured shoulder which gave her little chance of avenging her defeat at the Olympics.

There had been birthday celebrations during the visit: Nadia was 15 on 12 November and Teodora 16 the day after. A joint party had been arranged, with a splendid birthday cake provided by their Japanese hosts. To add to the excitement came the news that Nadia had been voted 'World Sportswoman of the Year' by the Sports Editors of the European Press. There seemed to be no end to the honours that were being heaped upon her for – with the triumphant return of the team to Romania – she was to hear that she had been invited to London to make a guest appearance on the television programme 'Sports Review of the Year' to receive the award of 'BBC Overseas Personality of 1976'. She was delighted to hear that the invitation had been accepted for her. For while the thought of having to say thank you in English in front of a vast audience was intimidating, the chance of a visit to London at Christmas time was wonderful! There would be the famous lights to see and the shops in which she would be able to buy super presents for everybody. A flight had been arranged for 14 December – the day before the programme was to be televised 'live'. I went to the airport to meet her with Cristian Constantinescu, the Cultural Secretary from the Romanian Embassy. Paul Lang, the producer of the programme, and Tony Murdoch of the British Amateur Gymnastics Association were also there to welcome her with flowers.

Returning from Heathrow to the Royal Garden Hotel, we found Frank Taylor of the *Daily Mirror*, who had witnessed her first triumph in England at the Champions All Contest in 1975, also waiting for her. But the young VIP looked pale and tired, and we remembered what a long day she must have had – Romanian time being two hours ahead of English. Nadia was stifling her yawns as she posed for the *Mirror* photographer, and was obviously only too glad to be sent off to bed by Nicolae Vieru, Secretary General of the Romanian National Council of Physical Education and Sports, who had accompanied her.

Next day she had a tight schedule – a morning reception at the Romanian Embassy, photographs with me in Kensington Gardens and an afternoon rehearsal at the BBC. Nevertheless every spare

Nadia receiving the BBC Television award.

moment had her rushing off to do her Christmas shopping – except for the odd minutes when I was able to tie her down to sort through a collection of pictures for this book.

At lunch-time she ordered carefully, concentrating on the proteins and vegetables of which her diet is composed. She ordered chicken, spinach and a green salad. But it was so long coming that I saw her casting envious eyes at the succulent Scotch steak that had been placed in front of Nicolae Vieru. Taking up her fork, she enjoyed the bit he offered her, and came back for more . . .

We were just rehearsing her little speech in English when a mouth-watering selection of dessert was wheeled towards us on a trolley. Nadia glanced at it disdainfully and with an enjoinder to her escort to choose the fresh fruit salad, she left us for a short rest and her daily exercises.

The hours flew by so that it seemed no time at all before the evening saw her sitting sedately at the side of John Curry – the Olympic Skating Gold Medallist who had headed the list of nominees for the British Award. A film of her Olympic triumphs called for warm applause which was redoubled as she stepped forward to receive her

Into the future

trophy from Clare Francis, the lone sailor. Then came the ordeal with the English that she understands so much better than she speaks. She had been apprehensive but she did splendidly.

'I am very thankful to the BBC and my English friends,' she said. 'I wish you all a Happy New Year.'

Next day she returned to Bucharest with the precious award, Christmas gifts for all the family and the game of Mastermind – in ten different languages – which I knew she would enjoy.

There was to be little respite for Bela and Marta Karoly during the brief holiday that saw the end of a momentous year and the ringing in of 1977. The world fame that the Gimnastica in Gheorghiu-Dej had won under their direction had inevitably created an increased burden of responsibilities, not least of which is the constant individual care that a girl with star quality must receive if she is to reach her potential. An ever-increasing amount of talent is emerging from the carefully selected 'tinies', and many of them, though still very young, have achieved high honours in the National Contests. They are the gymnasts among whom Bela and Marta expect to find their future stars.

Of first importance at the opening of the new spring term was the tour that had been planned for the USA. The team, of course, was to include Nadia who, with the American star Kathy Howard, would be the main attraction at New York's Madison Square Garden. But it was here that fate stepped in. For some weeks Bela and Mrs Mili had been concerned for Nadia's health and well-being. Now what had been a niggling worry suddenly flared as serious anxiety. It was not only her gymnastics but the constant strain of being in the limelight as a world celebrity that her doctors declared was proving too much for her adolescence. They were adamant that, while she was not to be denied routine practice, she was to be kept strictly away from competitions for at least three months. Much to everyone's disappointment it was reluctantly decided that the whole venture must be cancelled. Nadia was glad that Teodora would not be going without her.

So it was back to that pre-Olympic period, when there had been only school, the Gimnastica and home. Best of all for Nadia was to be once again in her own environment and away from the public eye.

But in March, as Teodora was concentrating on the defence of her *Daily Mirror* Champions All title, which she was to contest at Wembley on 16 April, Bela noticed that Nadia was becoming restless. Her health had greatly improved and it had been decided that

Into the future

Nadia in London, 1977

Elena Mukhina, left, and Nadia Comaneci. A display of grace masks a steely contest.

she would be able to defend her European title in Prague in mid-May. The contest was already exciting considerable interest throughout the world, and top gymnasts, particularly in the Eastern European countries, were putting everything into their training.

Mrs Mili, too, sensed Nadia's preoccupation and her need to test her prowess in an atmosphere other than the familiar arena of the Gimnastica – and with judges other than those to whom she was accustomed to assess the value of her disciplines. It had already been decided that she could go to France in early April to give a demonstration with Teodora and Georgeta. But that was not enough. Nadia needed a challenge to renew her competitive impetus.

Suddenly Bela – or it could have been Mrs Mili – found the answer. How would it be if she could be allowed to perform at Wembley in the Champions All Contest – which in Bela's

128

estimation ranks with the best in the world? Not as a competitor since the ruling permits only two gymnasts – one of either sex – to be sent from countries who have been invited to be represented. But as a guest who would be marked by the judges solely to test her reaction after her enforced rest.

They put it to the Competition Organisers who – pleased with the thought of how happy the young audience would be to see the famous little champion as an undreamed-of bonus – were glad to agree. But it presented problems for Tony Murdoch, the indefatigable BAGA Coordinator, who, in a single afternoon, had to allow for the March On of the gymnasts following the exciting opening of a fanfare from the Band of Life Guards, the introduction of the twenty young contestants and their work on the apparatus, the March Off and the Presentation. The whole had to fit in with BBC Television and finish

Into the future

to include Nadia's disciplines and an individual presentation. But with the ovation she received it certainly proved to be a happy decision, with only the long distance coach drivers disgruntled at leaving an hour late!

It is nice to record that Teodora retained her title without difficulty. She is a favourite indeed, in England, and everyone will be glad to see her back. Now her immediate challenge was to go with Nadia, the defending European champion, to Prague.

Gymnasts the world over were looking forward to Nadia and Teodora fighting for supremacy against Nelli Kim – who had won the Olympic silver – and Elena Mukhina, a brilliant 16 year-old star who has recently come to shine in the Soviet firmament. Remarkable for her skill and courage in being the first gymnast to perform a forward somersault on the beam, Elena is seen by many as Nadia's most formidable potential rival in the years to come.

Such an important contest might have been a happy note on which to end the postscript I have written to bring Nadia's career up to date. But it was not to be! For soon after the Prague contest had started, a questionable discrepancy in the judges' marking was to cause havoc. The audience in the arena was bewildered, and no one was certain in the chaotic confusion who would be standing as winners on the rostrum . . .

For the millions upon millions of enthusiasts who were seeing it on television, the culminating disappointment came with the announcement that was made in several languages immediately before the final contest on the floor, when Nadia was leading in the overall total.

'Nadia and Teodora have left the arena,' the announcer told us. 'They are no longer in the stadium.' After a formal appeal from Bela to the judges against Nadia's low marking, a telephone call had been received from Bucharest instructing the Romanian team to withdraw.

To say that it caused a sensation is an understatement. Newspapers and television and radio stations all over the world gave it elaborate coverage, and it made headlines in the Romanian press for four consecutive days. In a letter I received from Katsu Moriyama, he writes of the concern that is felt in Japan, and of their hopes that the promised enquiry that is to be held by the Federation of International Gymnastics will result in a foolproof system – one that will allow the contestants to compete with a renewed confidence in their judges in time for the approaching World Championships and the Moscow Olympics.

Into the future

My main concern has been to obtain an unbiased consensus of opinion as to how Nadia *really* performed in Prague. I consulted only those who were qualified to assess it. One of them had been present in the arena and the others – themselves gymnastic judges – had sat together to view the competition on television. It was interesting that each of the latter had used the International Code of Points in making the individual assessments. Without a single exception it was considered that Nadia's disciplines had been better even than those which won her perfect 10's at the Olympics. Her vault was judged to be one of the best she has ever done and her movements on the bar superb – both in choice and fluency of execution. Everyone to whom I spoke was outraged at her low marking.

But wherever I went I found the overriding hope that the whole unfortunate happening will be settled so that it can be forgotten.

We all hope so. Not only for ourselves but for all these exquisitely graceful girls of every nationality who enthrall us with their courage and dedication to what Mrs Mili has so aptly described in her Foreword as 'a beautiful sport'.

Picture Credits

The author would like to thank all those who have helped with illustrations for this book, and in particular Ion Mihaica, Peter Moeller and Aurel Neagu for many superb pictures.

Vasile Bageac, pages 37 top; BBC Copyright 125; C. Bursuc 43 top, 47, 70, 71 top, 80, 83; Foto CPCS 32 top; Nelu Gheorghilas 26; Atanasia Ionescu-Albu 78–9, 106–7; Peter Kinnear 120; E. Lacey, 76; *International Gymnast*: title page; Ion Mihaica 10, 13, 20, 24–5, 27, 31, 32 below, 52–3, 57, 71 below, 87 top, 89, 91, 96–7, 114, 116–7, 119, 123; Peter Moeller 40, 44, 48–9, 55, 62–9, 73–4, 104–5, 108, 109 top, 111, 127, 129; National Film Board of Canada 8; Novosti 109 below, 110; Paul Popper 103; Bakcsy Sigmund 23, 59, 118 top; *Sport* 87 below left, 113 below; *Sportul* 37 below, 99; Sundby Sports Inc 85; Tass 128.

MONTREAL OLYMPICS 1976

FLOOR EXERCISES

		Compulsory	Optional	Preliminary	Final	Total
gold	Nelli Kim (USSR)	9.80	9.90	9.85	10.00	19.850
silver	Ludmila Tourischeva (USSR)	9.90	9.95	9.925	9.90	19.825
bronze	Nadia Comaneci (Rom)	9.75	9.85	9.80	9.95	19.750
	Anna Pohludkova (Czech)	9.65	9.80	9.725	9.85	19.575
	Marion Kische (E. Ger)	9.65	9.70	9.675	9.80	19.475
	Gitta Escher (E. Ger)	9.70	9.70	9.70	9.75	19.450

THE BEAM

		Compulsory	Optional	Preliminary	Final	Total
gold	Nadia Comaneci (Rom)	9.90	10.00	9.950	10.00	19.950
silver	Olga Korbut (USSR)	9.80	9.85	9.825	9.90	19.725
bronze	Teodora Ungureanu (Rom)	9.75	9.85	9.80	9.90	19.700
	Ludmila Tourischeva (USSR)	9.40	9.85	9.625	9.85	19.475
	Angelika Hellmann (E. Ger)	9.50	9.60	9.550	9.90	19.450
	Gitta Escher (E. Ger)	9.50	9.65	9.575	9.70	19.275

THE VAULT

		Compulsory	Optional	Preliminary	Final	Total
gold	Nelli Kim (USSR)	9.80	9.90	9.85	9.95	19.800
silver	Ludmila Tourischeva (USSR)	9.80	9.80	9.80	9.85	19.650
bronze	Carloa Dombeck (E. Ger)	9.60	9.90	9.75	9.90	19.650
	Nadia Comaneci (Rom)	9.70	9.85	9.775	9.85	19.625
	Gitta Escher (E. Ger)	9.70	9.80	9.75	9.80	19.550
	Marta Egervari (Hung)	9.70	9.70	9.70	9.75	19.450

ASYMMETRIC BARS

		Compulsory	Optional	Preliminary	Final	Total
gold	Nadia Comaneci (Rom)	10.00	10.00	10.00	10.00	20.000
silver	Teodora Ungureanu (Rom)	9.90	9.90	9.90	9.90	19.800
bronze	Marta Egervari (Hung)	9.85	9.90	9.875	9.90	19.775
	Marion Kische (E. Ger)	9.90	9.90	9.90	9.85	19.750
	Olga Korbut (USSR)	9.90	9.90	9.90	9.40	19.300
	Nelli Kim (USSR)	9.80	9.85	9.825	9.40	19.225

SCORES IN THE FINAL

THIS IS HOW THE TOP SIX GIRLS FINISHED	Preliminary Scores	Vault	Bars	Beam	Floor	Total	Final Scores
Nadia Comaneci (Rom)	39.525	9.85	10.00	10.00	9.90	39.75	79.275
Nelli Kim (USSR)	39.125	10.00	9.90	9.70	9.95	39.55	78.675
Ludmila Tourischeva (USSR)	39.125	9.95	9.80	9.85	9.90	39.50	78.625
Teodora Ungureanu (Rom)	39.025	9.75	9.90	9.90	9.80	39.35	78.375
Olga Korbut (USSR)	38.975	9.80	9.90	9.50	9.85	39.05	78.025
Gitta Escher (E. Ger)	38.800	9.90	9.85	9.55	9.65	38.95	77.750